Stories

of Early Christianity

Creative Retellings of Faith and History

vanThanh Nguyen, SVD, SThD

Liguori
LIGUORI, MISSOURI

Imprimi Potest:
Harry Grile, CSsR, Provincial
Denver Province, The Redemptorists

Published by Liguori Publications
Liguori, Missouri 63057

To order, call 800-325-9521
liguori.org

Library of Congress Cataloging-in-Publication Data

Nguyen, vanThanh, 1965-
  Stories of early Christianity : creative retellings of faith and history / vanThanh Nguyen.
     pages cm
  1. Bible stories, English—N.T. Acts. 2. Church history—Primitive and early church, ca. 30-600. I. Title.
  BS2625.55.N48 2013
  226.6'09505—dc23
                                                                          2013007003

p ISBN: 978-0-7648-2323-7

e ISBN: 978-0-7648-6858-0

Liguori Publications, a nonprofit corporation, is an apostolate of The Redemptorists. To learn more about The Redemptorists, visit Redemptorists.com.

Printed in the United States of America
17 16 15 14 13 / 5 4 3 2 1
First Edition

Dedicated to
several exemplary Christian couples
and good friends:

Khiêm & Nhung

Khai & Huyền

Lĩnh & Nghệ

Lucy-Xuyến & Joe Kissane

Table of Contents

Sidebars

Biblical Characters

Biblical Backgrounds

Acknowledgments

This book started out as a five-day retreat that I gave to the Capuchin Franciscan community in the summer of 2011 at Monte Alverno Retreat Center in Appleton, Wisconsin. Capuchin Ed Foley took a huge risk when he asked me to direct their provincial retreat that year. Being young and not knowing what I was getting myself into, I accepted the invitation without hesitation. However, it is sometimes a foolish yes that pays great dividends in the end. I am deeply grateful to Ed for his encouragement.

I am deeply grateful to many people for their constant support and help. I would like to express the deepest appreciation to two SVD confreres, Stan Uroda and John Fincutter, who carefully read over the manuscript and offered good editorial suggestions. Stan has a laser-sharp eye for noticing the fine grammatical details that I often overlooked, and John has incredible patience to check for doctrinal and theological inconsistencies. I sincerely thank the SVD community at East Troy, Wisconsin, for their camaraderie and hospitality. Much of this book was written while I was staying at their lovely place overlooking Lake Beulah. I would like to name especially Father Ed Peklo, the rector of the community, who was most gracious in giving me the best room in the house. I am also grateful to Christy Hicks, acquisition editor at Liguori Publications, for her support and assistance in completing this project.

Last but not least, I would like to thank Catholic Theological Union (CTU) for allowing me to go on sabbatical, and the Provincial of the Chicago Province, Rev. Tom Ascheman, and his council members for making it possible by their support. I am therefore grateful to both CTU and the Society of the Divine Word for allowing me time off from my teaching responsibilities to research and write.

November 22, 2012
Thanksgiving Day

Introduction

You think you know the origins of early Christianity. Perhaps you are familiar with the acts of Peter and the missionary journeys of Paul, but do you realize that the stories of early Christianity contain many more stories than those of these two apostles of the Church? Deeds are performed by other courageous and faith-filled disciples (women as well as men) whom many Christians are completely unaware of.

Stories of Early Christianity recounts ten important events found in Acts of the Apostles. In what I hope is an engaging and imaginative style, this book allows mostly unknown characters to tell their stories of the early Church. They will show how they fit into the overall plan of God and how their acts of strength, courage, perseverance, and faith can inspire the lives of everyday believers. These characters are ordinary individuals who are open to the guidance of the Holy Spirit and thus become remarkable "friends of God" (*theophiloi*).[1] The aim is to retell the biblical stories in ways that allow readers to be drawn into the stories, identify themselves with the biblical characters, and be transformed in the act of reading and meditation.

The characters who narrate their own experience are Mary, Matthias, Rhoda, John Mark, Cornelius, Barnabas, Lydia,

....

[1] The author of both the Gospel of Luke and Acts of the Apostles addressed a certain person named *theophilos*, which means "friend of God" or "beloved by God" (Luke 1:3; Acts 1:1). Since Luke referred to him as "most excellent" (Luke 1:3), some scholars suggest that he was a Roman official or patron who had commissioned the author to write the Gospel and Acts. Other scholars, however, suggest the name is simply a literary construction to represent anyone who is loved by God or a friend of God.

Dionysius the Areopagite, Priscilla and Aquila, and Luke. Though these stories are "imaginative retellings," they remain true to the spirit of the person revealed in the Acts of the Apostles. They are actually narratives of faith and history. Furthermore, by entering into their story world, we will be able to unravel some of the mysteries that have eluded us for so long. For example: What did Jesus do and say during the forty days between resurrection and ascension? Where was the upper room located, and what really happened there at Pentecost? Who was the first gentile convert? What was the Jerusalem Council really about? Who was the first European believer, and what could Paul have said that made the person believe in Jesus Christ? Who actually founded the churches in Corinth and Ephesus? Why did Paul and Barnabas go their separate ways? What did Paul say at the Areopagus that led to both failure and success?

Stories of Early Christianity has ten chapters. Each contains a creative retelling of a biblical event, a reflection on a key trait of a healthy spirituality drawn from the biblical story, and a list of points for personal meditation or group sharing. It also includes two sidebars, one highlighting relevant biblical background and the other capturing important features of the biblical character of the chapter. In general, the book focuses on the miraculous and unpredictable working of the Holy Spirit in the lives of real people who are saints as well as sinners and who in various ways mirror the lives of all Christians.

As an Asian-American biblical scholar, a missionary, and an experienced retreat master, I hope this book will encourage readers to allow God to speak to specific circumstances in their lives through the biblical characters. Furthermore, it is my fervent prayer that this book help readers to grow in their relationship with God and achieve a healthy Christian spirituality.

Chapter 1 focuses on the character of Mary as a model of patience. Since Mary, the Mother of Jesus, was present during the forty days between the resurrection and ascension, she tells the story of the Church's new and humble beginnings. Her story will inspire readers to "be still" to enter the forty days of sacred time.

Chapter 2 explores Matthias, whom I call "Lucky Thirteenth." As the newest member of the apostolic band, Matthias recounts the tumultuous days between ascension and Pentecost and how he was chosen to be the thirteenth apostle. His story invites readers to reflect on their own vocational discernment and on prayer as an essential staple of the Christian life.

Chapter 3 describes the day of Pentecost. In an interview given by Luke, the author of the third Gospel and Acts, Rhoda—a young maid in the house of Mary, the mother of John Mark (Acts 12:12–13)—reveals the details that remarkable day in the upper room in Jerusalem. The reflection reminds Christians that we are to imitate Rhoda, the joyful servant, as cheerful Easter people.

Chapter 4 explores these questions: What was life really like in the earliest days of the Church? Was the community really of one heart and mind and without conflicts? John Mark gives the reader a more realistic account of the Church's fellowship, or *koinonia*. Furthermore, his reconciliation with Paul teaches us that forgiveness is a hallmark of authentic Christian love.

Chapter 5 turns to a Roman centurion who is a "faith-seeker" to relate the watershed story of his conversion and the Church's mission. The event is also known as "the gentile Pentecost." Cornelius's eagerness to hear the Word and be changed is a valuable lesson for all of us.

Next, the Jerusalem Council indicates that the early Church struggled with the issue of gentile inclusion and mission. How did the early Church resolve this crisis that could have destroyed its unity? In **Chapter 6**, Barnabas, who witnessed the event, tells his side of the story about resolving the controversy. Barnabas, whose name means "the son of encouragement," demonstrates that encouragement can be an important ministry, for it gives comfort, like that of the Holy Spirit, who is called "the Comforter."

In **Chapter 7**, Paul and his companions are impelled to cross into Europe. At Philippi, Paul spoke to a group of women and converted the first European believer, Lydia. Filled with gratitude, she generously opens her home to Paul and his traveling companions. Her spirit of gratitude that led to generous hospitality teaches us that thankfulness is an important Christian virtue.

Paul's speech at the Areopagus is one of the most powerful sermons found in Acts. In **Chapter 8**, Dionysius unveils the meaning of the speech and how it led to his conversion. His story also teaches that success or failure in ministry depends a lot on a person's tolerance of diversity.

Chapter 9 examines the best-known married couple in the New Testament. Priscilla, the migrant missionary "apostle," relates her story of exile and how together with Aquila, her husband, collaborated with Paul to found the churches in Corinth and Ephesus. Her story highlights the Gospel value of friendship in ministry.

In **Chapter 10** the author of Acts, Luke, tells readers who he is and why he wrote Acts of the Apostles. From his writings, we discover a healthy person who knows how to balance work and leisure.

This book is intended for a wide audience. It is designed for pastors, teachers, and catechists. Retreatants may find the book very inspirational. Bible students may be surprised to find that these stories are not simply pious reflections but may open their minds to a fascinating and informative reading of the Acts of the Apostles. The work as a whole offers the reader a solid introduction to Acts and to its author, Luke. It can serve as a helpful resource for retreat masters and also preachers. The chapters are enhanced with a list of discussion points that could make this an interesting resource for parish Bible-study groups.

Stories of Early Christianity attempts to capture the spiritual journey of every believer or "friend of God" (*theophilos*). The book creatively retells stories of famous as well as ordinary individuals who in various ways mirror you and me. Every one of us can identify with many of these biblical characters. As you read and reflect on these amazing stories of faith and the history of the early Church, allow yourself to be drawn into them as they will, in many ways, describe your own journey of faith.

The Church's New Beginnings

Every ending is a new beginning. All beginnings are adventurous and exciting and require much patience. Acts of the Apostles tells the story of the Church's new and humble beginnings. Having witnessed the resurrected Christ, the disciples were no longer the same frightened followers. They began to see with a new set of eyes, hear with attentive ears, and feel with a compassionate heart. Though Luke does not explicitly name those who were present at the scene of the ascension, we can certainly imagine that Mary, the Mother of the Lord, and other women followers were present along with the disciples. Since Mary probably witnessed the events during the forty days between the resurrection and ascension, let us hear about the new beginnings of the Church from her words. Allow her story to inspire you to enter this sacred time and to practice the spirituality of patience in times of restlessness. But first, pause to read Acts 1:1–11:

> In the first book, Theophilus, I dealt with all that Jesus did and taught until the day he was taken up, after giving instructions through the holy Spirit to the apostles whom he had chosen. He presented himself alive to them by many proofs after he had suffered, appearing to them during forty days and speaking about the kingdom of God. While meeting with them, he enjoined them not to depart from Jerusalem, but to wait for "the promise of the Father about which you have heard me speak; for John baptized with water, but in a few days you will be baptized with the holy Spirit." When they had gathered

together they asked him, "Lord, are you at this time going to restore the kingdom to Israel?" He answered them, "It is not for you to know the times or seasons that the Father has established by his own authority. But you will receive power when the holy Spirit comes upon you, and you will be my witnesses in Jerusalem, throughout Judea and Samaria, and to the ends of the earth." When he had said this, as they were looking on, he was lifted up, and a cloud took him from their sight. While they were looking intently at the sky as he was going, suddenly two men dressed in white garments stood beside them. They said, "Men of Galilee, why are you standing there looking at the sky? This Jesus who has been taken up from you into heaven will return in the same way as you have seen him going into heaven."

Mary, the Patient Mother

My name is Mary from Nazareth. I now live on Mount Zion in Jerusalem where my Son's followers assemble daily to break bread and go to the Temple to pray. A few other women who followed him around from Galilee to Jerusalem are also here with me. These women are incredibly courageous. They stuck with Jesus until the very end while the male disciples fled in fear during his arrest and crucifixion. I cannot tell you how exciting and wonderful these forty days are, considering what happened before. This is a sacred and precious time for all of us. Imagine spending forty days with the risen Christ.

Most of the male disciples have come back to the fold, but some are still afraid of the authorities. As a result, we still lock our doors and keep a low profile. Nevertheless, we gather in the upper room every day to pray and to recall those wonderful memories of my Son. During these days, Jesus has appeared to be with his disciples and to teach them. They hang on to every word that comes from his mouth. His instructions and explanations make more sense now. I can see the excitement and joy in the eyes of his disciples. Jesus is preparing them for something extraordinary that is going to happen soon. He talks much about the promise of the Holy Spirit that will empower them to be witnesses to him from Jerusalem to Samaria and even to the ends of the earth. It is truly an exciting new beginning.

But let me begin with that memorable Sunday morning when the news began to spread among the women and the disciples that the body of Jesus was missing from the tomb. The news was incredulous for all of them. They had recalled his predictions about being raised up on the third day, but such a thing was impossible to comprehend, let alone to believe. But deep down in my heart, I knew he would. As soon as Mary Magdalene had told her story of what happened at the tomb, I believed. Gradually one disciple after another began to tell their versions of experiencing the risen Christ. They all testify to the same thing—Jesus is alive.

Sidebar 1.1
Biblical Characters

Who is...*Mary of Nazareth?*

❖ Mary, or *Miriam* in Hebrew, was a Jewish woman who was betrothed to Joseph. She, however, conceived by the Holy Spirit and gave birth to Jesus, who was the Messiah or Christ. Because of her special status, she is also called the Blessed Virgin Mary and the Mother of God. Church tradition from early nonbiblical writings (like the Gospel of James) relates that her parents were an elderly couple named Joachim and Anne.

❖ Various New Testament writings record Mary's role in key events of the life of Jesus from his conception to his ascension. While not found in the canonical writings, apocryphal writings tell of her subsequent death and bodily assumption into heaven.

❖ The Catholic Church has several Marian dogmas and doctrines, such as the Immaculate Conception of Mary (on December 8, 1854, by Pope Pius IX) and the Assumption of Mary (on November 1, 1950, by Pope Pius XII). Most Protestants do not share these beliefs.

❖ Mary's most memorable words are expressed in her *Magnificat* (Lk 1:46–55).

And indeed he was appearing to the disciples during these forty days. Everyone was overjoyed to see him again.

During these forty days, Jesus opens the Scriptures to them and explains that things had to happen the way they did to fulfill the ancient prophecies. Jesus particularly instructs them about the kingdom of God. Sometimes the disciples ask Jesus questions. One was about the time of the restoration of Israel. To this, Jesus simply replies, "It is not for you to know the times and periods that the Father has set by his own authority" (Acts 1:7). Jesus and his disciples carried on many conversations, often into the late hours of the night. Jesus knew how important these "forty days" were. He, too, had spent forty nights and days in the wilderness where he was "tempted by the devil" (Luke 4:2) before he embarked on his mission. Similarly, Moses spent forty days on Mount Sinai before receiving God's Law (Exodus 34:28) as did Elijah on Mount Horeb (1 Kings 19:8) before beginning his prophetic ministry. The disciples, too, needed this sacred time to receive special guidance and preparation for the work of ministry that lay ahead. In reality, the disciples are given a second chance with Jesus. They had missed many important things the first time around, and they want to ensure it won't happen again. They are attentive, hanging on his every word and not wasting this precious second opportunity to be with him and learn from him.

It is difficult to fully describe the joy and the spirit of the disciples during these forty days. It is like being on a vision quest or, to put it in your terminology, a spiritual exercise where people withdraw from the busyness and pressures of the world to be with God and to seek God's guidance for the tasks at hand. I hope and pray that as you read, reflect, and pray over the stories of these friends of God in the Acts of the Apostles, you too will experience Christ's presence and be filled with the gifts of the Holy Spirit to begin a new day.

To be honest, I wish these forty days would stretch to fifty, sixty, or even longer, but I know that is not possible. After forty days of preparation, Jesus knows his time has come to depart from this world—not by means of death but, rather, ascension into heaven. As Jesus is lifted up, the disciples watch in awe and disbelief. Their faces show great sadness, for he has now departed from them for the second and final time. Yet they are also filled with great joy, for Jesus is now ascended into heaven to be seated at the right hand of God. With his ascension, Jesus is now gloriously affirmed as God's Son and the Messiah. While it is difficult to comprehend theologically and impossible to conceive physically, the ascension of Jesus is one of the central tenets of faith that Christians profess when they recite the Creed: "He ascended into heaven and is seated at the right hand of the Father." Jesus is now duly enthroned in his proper place. He was from God and has returned to God where he rightfully belongs.

Sidebar 1.2
Biblical Backgrounds

What is…*the ascension?*

❖ The ascension of Jesus is the New Testament teaching that the resurrected Jesus was taken up to heaven in the presence of his disciples forty days after his resurrection. The account of Jesus' ascending bodily into the clouds is briefly described in the Gospel of Luke (24:50–53) but is more fully narrated in Acts of the Apostles (1:9–11). The longer ending of the Gospel of Mark (16:19) only alludes to this event.

❖ The Gospel of Luke states that the event took place "in the vicinity of Bethany," and Acts mentions that it took place on the Mount of Olivet. Early Christians honored the event in a cave on the Mount of Olives. Today, the Chapel of the Ascension, built on the traditional site, is a Christian and Muslim holy site, believed to mark the place where Jesus ascended into heaven. In the small round church (also a mosque) is a stone imprinted with what some claim to be the very footprints of Jesus.

❖ The feast of the ascension, which is one of the chief feasts of the Christian year and dates back to as early as the fourth century, is celebrated on the fortieth day of Easter (which is always on a Thursday) or the following Sunday.

It is indeed a glorious day. The disciples stand watching as Jesus disappears into the clouds. They are completely mesmerized. Their necks stretch upward, their eyes fixed on that point where Jesus vanishes into the sky. None of them want to look away. Suddenly two men in white robes appear and ask, "Why are you standing there looking at the sky?" The disciples finally awaken from their trance. They begin to realize they cannot keep staring into the sky, nor can they go back to their ordinary way of life. For forty days, they have been prepared for this day. Ascension is like the handoff when Jesus will pass on the baton to his followers to spread the Good News and to continue telling the story of the kingdom of God. The question is, Will they accept the challenge of continuing the work Jesus began or will they remain in doubt and fear? Realizing that the road ahead will be filled with many uncertainties, trials, and persecutions, the disciples brace themselves to be ready for anything. But what should they do next? They can't just stand on the Mount of Olivet looking toward the sky forever. Thus I suggest they go back to Jerusalem and wait as the Lord instructed them. I remind them that Jesus promised they would be filled with the power of the Holy Spirit, and so we go back to Jerusalem and wait.

"Being Still" in Times of Restlessness

To wait is to be still. But most people are restless and do not like to be still. Our culture has driven us to become busy, active beings. We live in a very fast-moving world. Our computers boot up in seconds. High-speed Internet allows us to have all kinds of information at our fingertips. News around the world is broadcast instantly. We rush to get to work and rush to get home. We have no time to waste, for time is money. Thus waiting at a traffic light can seem to last forever even though it is usually only a minute and thirty seconds. How often do we find ourselves standing in line or being stuck in traffic and mutter under our breath, "I don't have time for this!"

Waiting has become almost uncivilized in this era of hyper-speed. How many times have you stood in a line and almost burst a blood vessel fuming over some minor inconvenience? How many times have you seen people blowing up at friends, confreres, and family members; honking horns in traffic jams; having angry confrontations in public places? And don't forget the stampede to get off airplanes, the cursing at automated message systems, the lack of etiquette everywhere. All of these and many other societal problems can be traced back to impatience and restlessness.

Yet patience is a prominent theme in the Bible. In the Old Testament, patience is referred to in several places in the Book of Proverbs: "Long-suffering results in great wisdom; a short temper raises folly high" (14:29); "The ill-tempered stir up strife, but the patient settle disputes" (15:18); and "The patient are better than warriors, and those who rule their temper, better than the conqueror of a city" (16:32). This virtue is also discussed in other sections, such as Ecclesiastes: "Better is a patient spirit than a lofty one. Do not let anger upset your spirit, for anger lodges in the bosom of a fool" (7:8–9). The story of Micah, for example, is that he suffers many challenging conditions and yet endures, saying, "I will wait for God my savior; my God will hear me!" (7:7). Patience in God, it is said, will aid believers in finding the strength to be delivered from the evils inherent in this physical life. The psalmist says, "Be still and know that I am God!" (46:11a).

According to a traditional Hebrew story, Abraham was sitting outside his tent one evening when he saw an old man, weary from age and his journey, coming toward him. Abraham rushed out, greeted him, and then invited him into his tent. There he washed the old man's feet and gave him food and drink. The old man immediately began eating without saying any prayer or blessing. So Abraham asked him, "Don't you worship God?" The old traveler replied, "I worship fire only and reverence no other god." When he heard this, Abraham became angry, grabbed the old man by the shoulders, and threw him out of his tent into the cold night air. When the old man had departed, God called to his friend Abraham and asked where the stranger was. Abraham replied, "I forced him out because he did not worship you." God answered, "I have suffered him these eighty years although he dishonors me. Could you not endure him one night?"[2]

In the New Testament, patience is referred to in several places. In his First Letter to the Thessalonians, Saint Paul states that we should "be patient with all. See that no one returns evil for evil; rather, always seek what is good for each other and for all" (5:14b–15). In Galatians, patience is listed as one of the fruits of the Spirit: "love, joy, peace, patience, kindness, generosity, faithfulness, gentleness, self-control. Against such there is no law" (5:22–23). In the First Letter to Timothy, the author states that "Christ Jesus might display all his patience as an example for those who would come to believe in him for everlasting life" (1:16b). In the Letter of James, the author urges Christians to be patient: "See how the farmer waits for the precious fruit of the earth, being patient with it until it receives the early and the late rains. You too must be patient. Make your hearts firm, because the coming of the Lord is at hand" (5:7–8).

In the Christian religion, patience is one of the most valuable virtues of life. Increasing patience is viewed as the work of the Holy Spirit in the Christian who has accepted the gift of salvation. While patience is not one of the three theological virtues nor one of the four cardinal virtues, it is one of the seven traditional virtues, alongside chastity, temperance, charity, diligence, kindness, and humility.

Patience in Islam is one of the best and most valuable virtues

....

[2] Adapted from Thomas Lindberg, see bible.org/illustration/abraham (accessed May 1, 2013).

of life. Through patience, a Muslim believes that an individual can grow closer to God and thus attain true peace. Islam also stresses that God is with those who are patient, more specifically during suffering. Some of the Quran verses about patience urge Muslims to "seek God's help with patient perseverance and prayer" (2:45) and "give glad tidings to those who patiently persevere" (2:155–157). In Buddhism, patience is one of the "perfections" that a *bodhisattva* (a holy person) trains in and practices to realize perfect enlightenment.

Jesus was a very patient man. He lived quietly, away from the limelight, for thirty years in a little town called Nazareth in upper Galilee. We know practically nothing about these sacred years. He must have spent a lot of time praying and discerning. He must have asked a lot of questions about his identity and mission. What was he called to do and be and when must he begin? He must have learned how to overcome his restlessness to begin his mission and learned to be patient from his mother.

Mary was definitely a patient woman. After saying yes, Mary encountered one adversity after another. Her pregnancy jeopardized her relationship with Joseph, a man she loved. By saying yes to God, Mary put her reputation and life on the line, for in those days an unfaithful woman was ordinarily stoned to death. The birth of Mary's Son was fraught with hardship: the journey to Bethlehem during her ninth month of pregnancy; the birth in a cold, dark, smelly stable; the flight into Egypt, a foreign country. Later on, Mary suffered misunderstandings with her twelve-year-old son in the Temple. Years later, after Jesus began his public ministry, she witnessed the rise of his popularity and his subsequent rejection. When she received word of his arrest, she went to Jerusalem and stood by the cross while Jesus was executed as a common criminal. Mary encountered one adversity after another. She suffered, but she persevered. Her heart did not grow weary and restless. She pondered everything in her heart and waited patiently for God to work. Mary is a good model and example for all of us who need to practice patience in times of restlessness.

Points for Reflection

- How do you feel at this moment? Are you rested or somewhat fatigued? Relaxed or tense? Reluctant and resistant?

- The forty days from resurrection to ascension were described as "sacred time." What do you think is meant by the phrase "sacred time"? When are your sacred times? What makes them sacred?

- At the ascension, the apostles kept standing and looking up at the sky, but they were also chastised for just standing around. What do you think is most important, to be still or to be active?

- Waiting is not a strong virtue for many people. What are you waiting for and anxious about? Is there anything blocking you at this time from finding God?

From Ascension to Pentecost

A cts narrates stories of real people. In the previous chapter we heard Mary, the mother of Jesus, telling us about the beginnings of the Church. It was an exciting and curious time. For forty days, from resurrection to ascension, the disciples were able to spend quality time with their risen Jesus. But on ascension day, Jesus was taken up into heaven. They were not quite prepared for this moment. What were they to do now that their Lord was no longer around to advise them? Were they supposed to wait or start preaching?

Allow me to let Matthias, the newest member of the apostolic band, tell his side of the story, particularly how he was chosen to be the thirteenth apostle. The story of his selection can teach us a lot about prayer, which is an important trait for developing a healthy spirituality. Pause to read Acts 1:12–26 and ask, How does Matthias's story of election intersect with my own vocation?

> Then they returned to Jerusalem from the mount called Olivet, which is near Jerusalem, a sabbath day's journey away. When they entered the city they went to the upper room where they were staying, Peter and John and James and Andrew, Philip and Thomas, Bartholomew and Matthew, James son of Alphaeus, Simon the Zealot, and Judas son of James. All these devoted themselves with one accord to prayer, together with some women, and Mary the mother of Jesus, and his brothers. During those days Peter stood up in the midst of the brothers (there was a group of about one hundred and twenty persons in the

one place). He said, "My brothers, the scripture had to be fulfilled which the holy Spirit spoke beforehand through the mouth of David, concerning Judas, who was the guide for those who arrested Jesus. He was numbered among us and was allotted a share in this ministry. He bought a parcel of land with the wages of his iniquity, and falling headlong, he burst open in the middle, and all his insides spilled out. This became known to everyone who lived in Jerusalem, so that the parcel of land was called in their language 'Akeldama,' that is, Field of Blood. For it is written in the Book of Psalms: 'Let his encampment become desolate, and may no one dwell in it.' And: 'May another take his office.' Therefore, it is necessary that one of the men who accompanied us the whole time the Lord Jesus came and went among us, beginning from the baptism of John until the day on which he was taken up from us, become with us a witness to his resurrection." So they proposed two, Joseph called Barsabbas, who was also known as Justus, and Matthias. Then they prayed, "You, Lord, who know the hearts of all, show which one of these two you have chosen to take the place in this apostolic ministry from which Judas turned away to go to his own place." Then they gave lots to them, and the lot fell upon Matthias, and he was counted with the eleven apostles.

Matthias, the Prayerful Apostle

Matthias is my real name, but my friends call me "Lucky Thirteenth." Some say I was chosen purely by luck to be part of the apostolic band, but deep down I know it was the Holy Spirit who actually handpicked me. I'm no latecomer, for I was with Jesus from the very beginning of his public ministry. I was a younger man then, but I followed him around and hung on every word he said. Although I was not part of the inner circle of the Twelve Apostles, I was captivated by Jesus and his message, and so I and many others followed him around Galilee and up to Jerusalem. I witnessed many amazing miracles that Jesus performed. Since the very first day I met Jesus, I had wanted to be his disciple. And so here I was, gathered in the upper room in Jerusalem, with the other apostles and disciples. We had just come back from the Mount of Olives where we witnessed Jesus' ascension into heaven. We were instructed to wait.

Now I admit, I do not like to wait. Waiting seems too passive. I like to act and take charge. I wanted to say, "Let's plan, organize, and strategize our mission!" I wanted to go out immediately and start preaching. My heart was inflamed with zeal. I could hardly control myself. But instead we followed Mary's advice to wait and pray.

> **Sidebar 2.1**
> **Biblical Characters**
>
> ### Who is...*Matthias*?
>
> ❖ He is the apostle chosen by the remaining eleven apostles to replace Judas Iscariot.
>
> ❖ His selection as an apostle is unique since Jesus did not call him personally, for Jesus had already ascended to heaven. Joseph, called Barsabbas (also known as Justus), was also nominated but was not chosen. The method of selection was through the drawing of lots (Acts 1:23–26).
>
> ❖ Because Matthias was a follower from the very beginning, Clement of Alexandria suggested he must have been among the seventy-two disciples senty by Jesus in mission (Lk 10:1–11, 17).
>
> ❖ According to legend, St. Matthias was beheaded in the year 80. His feast day is celebrated May 14. He is the patron of carpenters and tailors.

Something was strange that wonderful day in the upper room. My heart was moved and my spirit was at peace. I found prayer very meaningful and comforting. Present were the eleven apostles, Mary and her relatives, as well as other women and men disciples. We were different in age and background. We were not from the same village or even clan, but we were united as one family. We prayed

Sidebar 2.2
Biblical Backgrounds

What is...*casting of lots?*

❖ Casting of lots as a means of determining God's will occurs frequently in the Old Testament.

❖ In the Book of Leviticus, God commands Moses, "[Aaron] shall cast lots to determine which [goat] is for the LORD and which for Azazel" (16:8). In the Book of Jonah, the desperate sailors cast lots to see who was responsible for the storm, and the lot fell on Jonah (1:7). Proverbs also teaches, "Into the bag the lot is cast, but from the LORD comes every decision" (16:33). There are many other biblical references, such as 1 Sm 14:42; Dt 18:10; 1 Chr 26:13.

❖ In the New Testament, all four Gospels tell of the soldiers at Jesus' crucifixion casting lots to see who would get his clothing (Mk 15:24; Mt 27:35; Lk 23:34; Jn 19:24). Another notable example occurs in Acts where the eleven remaining apostles cast lots to determine whether Matthias or Barsabbas (surnamed Justus) would be chosen to replace Judas.

❖ Depending on the location and customs, different means of casting were practiced to help with decision-making. They varied from polished sticks to bones, stones, coins, dice, and more.

together fervently. While praying, one apostle suddenly spoke up, saying that our group was incomplete. Jesus had picked twelve apostles for a purpose, but now that Judas, the betrayer, had met his fate in an awful death, we were down to eleven apostles. "We need a replacement!" someone said out loud. Then Peter, who had taken on the role of leader of the church in Jerusalem those days, immediately spoke up. He pointed out that the betrayal and death of Judas had to be fulfilled as foretold in the Scriptures. Furthermore, another has to take Judas's place. He suggested that the person should be someone who had been with the movement from the very beginning, specifically, during "the whole time the Lord Jesus came and went among us, beginning from the baptism of John until the day on which he was taken up from us." Everyone agreed this was a good idea and that the criterion for the selection was a wise one.

After a brief moment of prayer, the community suggested my friend and companion, Joseph called Barsabbas, whom we called Justus, for he was very upright and kind. If anyone deserved to be chosen, it was Justus. I would support him completely. When my name was brought forth, I was dumbfounded. I could not believe what I was hearing. *Who was I to be chosen to be among this elite group of apostles and pillars of the Church?* I pointed out to all that I was unworthy to be sent out. I'm no missionary, I told them. I gave all sorts of excuses, from being too young to being awkward in speech. But no one bought my argument. My name stayed on the list.

So I waited. The hardest part was the discernment process of the community. How can we know which one is chosen by the Spirit? How can we discern God's will? Again the community turned to prayer, saying, "You, Lord, who know the hearts of all, show which one of these two you have chosen to take the place in this apostolic ministry from which Judas turned away to go to his own place." After the community had prayed, it was time to cast lots. The practice of casting lots was used frequently in Israel and the ancient world to determine God's will. According to our understanding, everything happens for a purpose. Nothing is haphazard or simply by chance. Everything is determined by God. Casting lots, therefore, is the best way to determine God's will. The Book of Proverbs says, "Into the bag the lot is cast, but from the LORD comes every decision" (16:33).

So it was by lot that I was chosen to replace Judas Iscariot. I was honored but at the same time humbled by the selection. I gave God thanks for having chosen me to be sent out to preach the Good News. I also expressed my gratitude to the whole assembly for their support and encouragement. I asked for their prayers so that I might be faithful and zealous in my new vocation. When the community extended their hands to pray over me, I felt as if I had been given a burst of energy and strength. I no longer trembled with fear but, rather, was filled with peace and grace. I was congratulated by everyone. I remember embracing Mary who didn't say anything, but her smile said everything. Her joy was contagious. Peter and the other eleven joyfully welcomed me into their group. My friend Justus also congratulated me with sincere jubilation. It was one of the happiest moments of my life.

Prayer As Staple of Christian Life

When I want to teach the importance of prayer, I always tell the following story. A disciple approached his teacher, asking earnestly for help in prayer. Agreeing to help, the rabbi led the eager disciple to a shallow river and proceeded to dunk the disciple's head into the water. Thirty seconds passed, followed by another thirty. Suddenly gasping for air, the disciple jerked his head out of the water and looked at the rabbi with bewilderment. Then the rabbi said to his disciple, "Unless your desire for prayer is as determined as your desire for air, you will not succeed." [3]

To wait is to "be still," and by being still in prayer, one discovers God. We can explore many intersecting themes from the biblical reflection. One dominant and important spiritual theme is prayer. First, what is prayer? The old *Baltimore Catechism* says, "Prayer is the lifting up of our minds and hearts to God." While this is not a bad definition, it does not capture the full meaning and dynamic of prayer. Prayer is not simply talking to God, which is a one-way street. Authentic prayer is a dialogue between two interested friends: God and self. Thus, a better definition of prayer might be "a conversation with God." In prayer, we talk to God, and God shares with us, which is a two-way street. However, Melannie Svoboda points out that this definition is still inadequate, for prayer goes beyond mere talking. She says, prayer is "being in the presence of someone you love and who loves you." [4]

....

[3] This story is adapted from Wilkie Au, SJ, *By Way of the Heart: Toward a Holistic Christian Spirituality* (Mahwah, New York: Paulist Press, 1989), 86.

[4] Melannie Svoboda, SND, *Traits of a Healthy Spirituality* (Mystic, CT: Twenty-Third Publications, 1997), 88.

Svoboda's definition comes from two spiritual writers. Saint Thérèse of Lisieux wrote, "With me prayer is an uplifting of the heart; a glance towards heaven; a cry of gratitude and love, uttered equally in sorrow and in joy. In a word, it is something noble, supernatural, which expands my soul and unites it to God."[5] Catherine de Hueck Doherty wrote, "Prayer is love expressed in speech and in silence. To put it another way, prayer is the meeting of two loves: the love of God and our love." I think Svoboda's definition of prayer, which has its basis in both Saint Thérèse of Lisieux and Doherty, captures beautifully the spiritual quintessence of prayer.

Prayer has always been and continues to be an important Christian staple and practice. All four gospels devote time and space to the subject of prayer; however, the Gospel of Luke has more to say about prayer than the other three. For Luke, Jesus devotes much time both in prayer and teaching his disciples to pray, so much so that some even call Luke "the Evangelist of prayer."

Luke depicts Jesus as a person who prays frequently, especially at crucial moments in his life. Before beginning his ministry, he withdrew into the desert to pray and fast for forty days and nights (Luke 4:1–13). At baptism, while he is praying, the heavens open above him, and the Spirit descends upon him. Only Luke links prayer with the descent of the Spirit at Jesus' baptism (Luke 3:21–22). This is consistent with other references in which the Spirit is given in answer to prayer (Luke 11:2; 11:13; Acts 1:14). Perhaps the revelatory experience of the heavens opening in prayer inspires him to open the kingdom of heaven to others in his ministry. Luke noted that Jesus "would withdraw to deserted places to pray" (Luke 5:16). To respond

....

5 From Chapter X: The New Commandment of the *Story of a Soul* (*l'Histoire d'une Ame): The Autobiography of St. Thérèse of Lisieux*; see ccel.org/ ccel/therese/autobio.xviii.html (accessed May 1, 2013).

to the strain of so many who flocked to him, Jesus needed to retreat to quiet places to be in communion with God and "recharge" his human energy.

Jesus' retreating to pray, which is situated after the healing of the man with leprosy and just prior to his first major conflict with the scribes and Pharisees, accentuates both the regularity of Jesus' prayer life and his desire to spend time with God before he faces any sort of opposition. Before choosing the Twelve, Jesus spent the whole night in prayer (6:12). By recording this, the Evangelist wishes to highlight the momentous decision Jesus was about to make. Consequently, in prayer Jesus is able to recognize the mystery of these human beings who are unperceptive and fragile, yet accept them as they are and what they can become despite their obvious weaknesses and flaws.

Before asking his disciples the question concerning his true identity, namely, "Who do the crowds say that I am?" only Luke reports that Jesus was praying in seclusion (9:18). On the Mount of Transfiguration, Jesus also prays to the Father (9:28–29). As he is praying, Jesus' appearance is changed. His clothes become dazzling white. Everything in him becomes visible, transparent to God's splendor. In prayer, Jesus recognizes his divine quality. His true self appears, and his authentic being also becomes evident to his disciples. It is noted that this is the only time others actually saw Jesus praying. Before Peter's triple denial, Jesus makes a priestly intercession for Peter so that his "faith may not fail" and that he in turn may strengthen others (22:32).

Luke also shows us the human side of Jesus when he struggles to accept God's will in the Garden of Gethsemane. There Jesus kneels before his Father and prays, "Father, if you are willing, take this cup away from me; still, not my will but yours be done" (22:42). Jesus struggles to understand God's way and therefore finds it difficult to submit to God's will. But in prayer, Jesus is able to overcome his fear and learns what God requires of him. More important, in prayer he is able to put himself at God's disposal and surrender to God's will as a perfectly obedient son. In and through prayer, Jesus finds the strength to carry his cross without becoming bitter or hardened. It is interesting, however, that Jesus still needed an angel to strengthen him (22:43).

Jesus' prayer comes to a climax on the cross. On the cross he prays for those who are crucifying him, saying, "Father, forgive them, they know not what they do" (Luke 23:34). At the most agonizing moment of his life, Jesus turns to the Father and prays for his enemies as he dies on the cross. In prayer he is able to love and forgive even his murderers. He puts into practice what he teaches, saying, "Love your enemies, do good to those who hate you, bless those who curse you, pray for those who mistreat you" (6:27–28). Finally, Jesus' last breath is a prayer, "Father, into your hands I commend my spirit" (23:46). Jesus' last words actually come from Psalm 31, which pious Jews would use to express complete trust and confidence in God's protection. Jesus' endearing address to his Father as "Abba" (Daddy) shows that, even in death, he dares to call God his loving Father in whom he finds comfort, love, and security.

Besides practicing prayer in his own life, Jesus also taught others why one should pray as well as how one ought to pray. There are five main passages, which taken together offer a paradigm for prayer. The two parables about being persistent in prayer, namely, the parable of the friend at midnight (Luke 11:5–8) and that of the persistent widow (18:1–8), teach one *how* to pray. The Lord's Prayer (11:1–4) teaches one *what* to pray. And in the exhortation to be vigilant (21:36), Jesus teaches *why* one should pray persistently and always be on watch.

Given the importance of prayer, it is interesting to note that Luke, a literary genius, both opens and closes his gospel with instances of prayer. While Zechariah is in the Holy of Holies, the full assembly of people was praying outside (1:10). The last verse of Luke's Gospel, which recalls what was said in the beginning and serves as a bracket or a literary *inclusio*[6], describes the scene of Jesus' followers in the temple constantly praising God (24:53). In his gospel, Luke also uniquely records several characters praying: Zechariah's Canticle (1:68–79); Mary's *Magnificat* (1:46–55); and Simeon's prayer of thanksgiving (2:26–32).

Since Jesus is a model of prayer, the disciples are to imitate him to avoid temptation and overcome opposition. Luke's second volume, the Acts of the Apostles, records many direct and deliberate motifs of prayer parallel to those found in his gospel. Jesus prays at his baptism and receives the Holy Spirit (Luke 3:21–22); the apostles and their companions pray (Acts 1:14) before the descent of the Holy Spirit (Acts 2:1–4). Peter and John pray for the Samaritans that they too may receive the Holy Spirit. After the two apostles lay hands on them, the Holy Spirit descends (Acts 8:15–17). Jesus prays before choosing the Twelve (Luke 6:12); the early Church prays before selecting Matthias (Acts 1:24). Jesus prays for his murderers on the cross (Luke 23:34); Stephen, the first Christian martyr, cries out in a loud voice before dying, "Lord, do not hold this sin against them" (Acts 7:60).

Acts describes many instances in which the community turns to prayer for deliverance, healing, and missionary purposes. When the Church was persecuted by Herod Agrippa, executing James the son of Zebedee and imprisoning Peter, the Church resorted to prayer (12:1–5). Peter and the Church prayed for the raising of Dorcas from death (9:40). Paul, too, prayed for the healing

....

[6] *Inclusio* is a literary device based on a concentric principle, also known as bracketing or an envelope structure, which consists of creating a frame by placing similar material at the beginning and end of a section. A good example of an inclusion is found in Matthew's Sermon on the Mount. The section concerning the law or the prophets starts and ends with the expression "the law and the prophets" (Mt 5:17 and 7:12).

of Publius' father who had been suffering from intermittent attacks of gastric fever (28:8). The newly appointed elders in the churches at Derbe, Lystra, Iconium, and Pisidian Antioch were commended by prayer and fasting (14:23).

Luke wants to point out that appointments to the various tasks in ministry must be bound up with prayer. The acceptance of gentiles into the plan of God is closely linked with prayer. In the watershed story of the inclusion of the gentile mission, namely, the story of Peter and Cornelius, the motif of prayer runs deep at several levels. Cornelius is not only described as a god-fearer who is devout and has given alms to the Jewish people but also one who "constantly prayed to God." His prayers and generosity are said to have risen "in God's sight" (Acts 10:2–4). On the following day, while praying at midday, Peter received a vision that ultimately led him to go to the house of the gentile centurion to proclaim the Good News to Cornelius and his household (10:9–33). While Peter was still speaking, the Holy Spirit descended upon the gentiles, and they spoke in tongues, glorifying God (10:45–46). Paul, the Apostle to the gentiles, knows well that his whole missionary endeavor, particularly the mission to the gentiles, is the work of God's grace and divine purpose, which the Church can only accept and embrace through prayer (14:24–28).

Paul turned to prayer to find strength in times of danger and distress. On his way to Jerusalem, he had a rendezvous with the Ephesian elders and warned them of the imminent dangers. Luke reports that after this discourse, Paul "knelt down and prayed with them all. They were all weeping loudly as they threw their arms around Paul and kissed him, for they were deeply distressed that he had said that they would never see his face again" (Acts 20:36–38). In prayer, the apostle and the elders found comfort and consolation. Similarly, after spending seven days with the disciples in Tyre, the disciples there grew fond of Paul and tried to prevent him from going up to Jerusalem. Luke records that "all of them, women and children included, escorted us out of the city, and after kneeling on the beach to pray, we bade farewell to one another" (21:5–6).

Acts of the Apostles presents the Church and its members regularly engaging in prayer, whether it be in the Temple, in private homes and rooftops, in the fields, or on the beach. One could pray at set times or at any time really, even at odd hours of the day or night. Luke clearly shows that prayer is a vital aspect of the life for the Church and its believers. We have seen that Jesus not only taught about prayer but he particularly gave examples and set the standard for his followers. In prayer Jesus certainly came into contact with his true self and his mission. Prayer helped him to discover God's will and gave him the strength to face his task. It gave him the clarity to be able to speak rightly about God and the determination to continue in preaching and building up the kingdom of God. Just as the early Christian disciples followed the example and teaching of Jesus to be diligent in prayer, believers today should also seek to emulate Jesus in every way possible.

Points for Reflection

- Matthias was chosen by lot. How were you chosen? How did you respond to God's call? How does Matthias's story of election intersect with your own calling?

- The early Christian community was constantly devoted to prayer (Acts 1:14). What things are you devoted to? What things do you pray for? What happens to you when you pray?

- What new beginnings are you embarking on? Is there any decision you have to make these days? What graces do you need at this time in your life?

Pentecost

I once heard an interesting story. When Jesus Christ had finished his work on earth and had returned to heaven, the angel Gabriel met him and said, "Lord, may I ask what plans you have made for carrying on your work on earth?"

"I have chosen twelve men and some women," said Jesus. "They will pass my message on till it reaches the whole world."

"But," said the angel, "supposing these few people fail you, what other plans have you made?" Christ smiled and said, "I have no other plan because I am counting on them." [7]

The Lord counted on the disciples to be his witnesses "in Jerusalem, throughout Judea and Samaria, and to the ends of the earth" (Acts 1:8). To assist them in the work, Jesus breathed on them the Holy Spirit to strengthen them in their journey.

Pentecost is one of the most important events narrated in Acts. With the outpouring of the Holy Spirit, the Church is born. The timid disciples were no longer afraid. This experience had been foretold by John the Baptist in Luke 3:16; promised by the risen Jesus in Luke 24:49; and anticipated in Acts 1:4–5. To help us enter the story, Luke will interview an eyewitness of the event of Pentecost. Her name is Rhoda. She will tell us what actually happened that day in the upper room in Jerusalem. But first, pause to read Acts 2:1–12:

....

[7] This story is adapted from Anthony Castle, *A Treasure of Quips, Quotes, and Anecdotes for Preachers and Teachers* (Mystic, CT: Twenty-third Publications, 1998), 55.

When the time for Pentecost was fulfilled, they were all in one place together. And suddenly there came from the sky a noise like a strong driving wind, and it filled the entire house in which they were. Then there appeared to them tongues as of fire, which parted and came to rest on each one of them. And they were all filled with the holy Spirit and began to speak in different tongues, as the Spirit enabled them to proclaim.

Now there were devout Jews from every nation under heaven staying in Jerusalem. At this sound, they gathered in a large crowd, but they were confused because each one heard them speaking in his own language. They were astounded, and in amazement they asked, "Are not all these people who are speaking Galileans? Then how does each of us hear them in his own native language? We are Parthians, Medes, and Elamites, inhabitants of Mesopotamia, Judea and Cappadocia, Pontus and Asia, Phrygia and Pamphylia, Egypt and the districts of Libya near Cyrene, as well as travelers from Rome, both Jews and converts to Judaism, Cretans and Arabs, yet we hear them speaking in our own tongues of the mighty acts of God." They were all astounded and bewildered, and said to one another, "What does this mean?"

Rhoda, the Joyful Servant

I, Luke, have heard many stories about that day, that great event that changed the course of human history. It was ten days after the ascension and fifty days after Passover. Pentecost fell on the Jewish harvest festival of Shavuot (the Festival of Weeks), which commemorates God's giving the Ten Commandments at Mount Sinai fifty days after the Exodus. For Christians, the day the Holy Spirit was poured out on all those who were gathered in the upper room is the birthday of the Church. Unfortunately, I was not there to witness this life-changing event for so many people. However, in the process of writing my Gospel and the Acts of the Apostles, and according to my practice of investigating everything for accuracy, I had to interview various people who were there. I would like to share with you an eyewitness account of that grand day.

The following excerpt is an interview I had with a woman named Rhoda. Rhoda is now in her mid-sixties and recently immigrated to Antioch from Jerusalem. At the time of Pentecost, which was fifty years ago, Rhoda was just a young maid in the house of Mary, the mother of John Mark (Acts 12:12–13).

> **Sidebar 3.1**
> **Biblical Characters**
>
> ### Who is…*Rhoda*?
>
> ❖ Rhoda is a young maid in the house of Mary, the mother of John Mark.
>
> ❖ She is most remembered as the maid who left Peter standing at the door. After his miraculous escape from jail, Peter knocks at the door of Mary's house. Rhoda comes to answer. Recognizing Peter's voice, she is so moved with joy that she abandons Peter at the gate and runs inside to tell the others.
>
> ❖ Rhoda in Greek and Latin means "rose."

Luke: "Now, Rhoda, would you please tell me a little about yourself and the events of that great day."

Rhoda: "Well, my name is Rhoda, as you already know. Most people know me as the maid who left the Apostle Peter standing outside the gate after his harrowing escape. I was just a young girl then. I had heard about Peter—or "Uncle Rocky" as I used to call him—being thrown into prison. That night before he was put on trial and probably would have been sentenced to death, many of us got together at the house of Mary, the mother of John Mark, to pray for Peter. While we were praying fervently behind locked doors, someone banged on our door. We were terrified, for we thought it was the temple soldiers coming to arrest us also. When I went to check who the intruder might be, I immediately recognized Peter's voice. But I got a bit too excited. Silly me! Instead of letting him in, I ran back into the house to announce to everyone that Peter was standing outside at the gate. Since that day, everyone teases me as the girl who left Peter standing at the gate. It's funny now as I recall the story, but it wasn't then, for he could have been recaptured and thrown back into prison."

Luke: "What about the day of Pentecost?" interjected Luke. "Please tell me what happened that day."

Rhoda: "As a maid, my job was to greet all the visitors at the gate and take them to the upper room, which by the way, was the same room where Jesus had celebrated the Last Supper. A lot of people came to our house that day. There was Mary, the Mother of Jesus, along with James and his siblings; the "Twelve," including Matthias, the newly chosen apostle, who is also known as "Lucky Thirteenth"; and many other disciples who were unfamiliar to me. Many women were assembled as well, including Mary Magdalene, Martha and her sister Mary, Joanna the wife of Chuza, Susanna, and Mary my matron, just to name a few.

"I was lucky to be there when the miracle happened. I was summoned to the upper room to open the windows, for it was getting stuffy. As I was opening the windows, a sudden rush of violent wind flung the windows open wide and filled the entire house. As I looked, I saw something strangely resembling tongues of fire resting on top of their heads. They immediately began to speak in tongues and praise God in multiple languages, which I amazingly could understand even though I am not at all familiar with the different languages. There were great bursts of joy and excitement. I noticed that people's faces and complexions had changed since their arrival. They were now filled with peace, joy, and enthusiasm. They were no longer afraid but filled with confidence. Everyone seemed to have been instantly transformed. I really didn't understand then, but later I was told that it was the gifts of the Holy Spirit."

Luke: "So what did the disciples do after receiving the gifts of the Holy Spirit?"

Rhoda: "Well, the room was getting too hot with all those tongues of fire floating around. Plus their hearts were now enflamed, which they couldn't seem to contain. It started with Peter, who fearlessly rushed out of the house, proclaiming that the Lord Jesus had risen. 'Jesus from Nazareth is the Messiah and is alive!' he shouted. Then everyone followed him outside. Some went to the marketplace, others to the Temple, still others to the surrounding towns and villages. It was maddening and frightful. It was chaotic, but no one seemed to care. They were too elated to be afraid.

"Now at this time, the Jews were celebrating the harvest festival of Shavuot, and people from throughout the empire were staying in Jerusalem. There were Parthians, Medes, Elamites, Egyptians, Cretans, and Libyans. There were visitors from

---

Sidebar 3.2
Biblical Backgrounds

What is...*pentecost*?

❖ *Pente-koste,* or "the Fiftieth Day" (literally in Greek), is the Jewish harvest festival called *Shavuot,* or Festival of Weeks (literally in Hebrew), which commemorates God's giving the Ten Commandments at Mount Sinai fifty days after the Exodus.

❖ In ancient times, the grain harvest lasted seven weeks and was a season of gladness and joy (Jer 5:24; Dt 16:9–11; Is 9:2).

❖ According to Luke, as recorded in Acts of the Apostles, the Holy Spirit descended upon the disciples who gathered in the upper room, or the Cenacle, while celebrating the Jewish harvest festival called Pentecost (*Shavuot*). Consequently, for Christians, Pentecost became the birthday of the Church, commemorating the descent of the Holy Spirit found in Acts 2:1–13.

as far away as Rome, Mesopotamia, Cappadocia, Pamphylia, and Phrygia. Nevertheless, they all understood everything in their native language. Amazed and perplexed, they sneered and accused the disciples of being drunk. But how could it be? It was still early in the morning, and I certainly hadn't supplied them with any wine.

"I remember following Peter and the other apostles to the Temple. Lots of people were buying and selling goods at the gentile courts on that particular day, and it was a zoo there. But Peter raised his voice and spoke. His voice was like thunder that carried a great distance, causing everyone to be quiet and listen. He spoke with force, determination, and enthusiasm. He was so eloquent. I have never heard him speak like that before. We had teased him for being indecisive, for that is the reason we nicknamed him "Rocky." But on that day, Peter was firm and confident. He had wisdom and knowledge. I can't recall word for word what he said that day, but I do remember that he used a lot of citations from Scripture to prove that Jesus is the promised Messiah. I can still hear his thunderous words ringing in my ears right now as I speak. He began by quoting words from the prophet Joel, who prophesied about the last days in which God will pour out God's Spirit upon all flesh, and everyone will prophesy. He talked about how young men shall see visions, and old men shall dream dreams. If I am not mistaken, the passage is from the prophet Joel.

"Peter also pointed out that even King David spoke about Jesus as the Messiah and Lord. He recited various verses from Psalms 16, 110, and 132. Peter's knowledge of the Scripture was impressive. He clearly demonstrated that Jesus of Nazareth, who was filled with power and performed many signs and wonders, was clearly appointed by God. He was crucified and died, but God raised him up on the third day. All these things happened because it is part of God's great plan and design. Peter's final testimony was, 'Jesus, the one you had crucified, is truly both Lord and Messiah!'

"I was so proud of Peter. He stood tall and upright. He was incredibly bold and faithful! I can never forget that remarkable day. His first public speech stirred their hearts. Some of them shouted, 'What are we to do?' And Peter said, 'Repent and be baptized, every one of you, in the name of Jesus Christ for the forgiveness of your sins; and you will receive the gift of the holy Spirit!' (2:37–38). About three thousand people were converted on that single day. And it was only the beginning!"

Joy As Sign of Genuine Faith

William Barclay said, "A gloomy Christian is a contradiction of terms." And I think he is right. If Christians are genuinely an Easter people, we must radiate joy. I always liked that simple children's song:

I've got the joy, joy, joy, joy   And I'm so happy
Down in my heart   So very happy
Down in my heart   I've got the love of Jesus
Down in my heart   in my heart
I've got the joy, joy, joy, joy   And I'm so happy
Down in my heart   So very happy
Down in my heart to stay   I've got the love of Jesus
                                   in my heart.

Julian of Norwich said,
  "The greatest honor you can give to God is to live gladly because of the knowledge of his love. If our joy gives honor to God, then it is our duty to be joyful."

Teilhard de Chardin said,
  "Joy is the infallible sign of the presence of God."

Many psalms in the Old Testament express joy and happiness:

> "Even now my head is held high above my enemies on every side! I will offer in his tent sacrifices with shouts of joy; I will sing and chant praise to the LORD" (27:6).

> "Light dawns for the just, and gladness for the honest of heart. Rejoice in the LORD, you just, and give thanks at the remembrance of his holiness" (97:11–12).

> "This is the day the LORD has made; let us rejoice in it and be glad" (118:24)

The book of Proverbs speaks much about joy:

> "A glad heart lights up the face, but an anguished heart breaks the spirit" (15:13).

> "One has joy from an apt response; a word in season, how good it is!" (15:23).

> "A joyful heart is the health of the body, but a depressed spirit dries up the bones" (17:22).

If joy is such an important element of our Christian spirituality, why do most people see faith only as serious business? For many, smiling has no place in church, community, or spirituality. But joy is a hallmark of our Christian faith. John Henry Newman once said, "The chief grace of primitive Christianity was joy!"

We might ask, then, why do we not smile more in church? Why is there a strain of gloom in Christianity and in our own spirituality? Why, for example, do the pictures of Jesus almost never show him smiling? After all, Jesus was someone who knew how to have a good time. He worked his first miracle at a wedding reception. He frequently dined in people's homes. Jesus was incredibly approachable. People of both genders and all ages flocked to him, including little children. And as we know, most children (as well as adults) are naturally drawn to happy, upbeat individuals. Joy was a major theme of Jesus' parables, while his principal image for the kingdom of God was a festive party.

The Gospel of Luke particularly accentuates the motif of joy, even more so than the other gospels. Luke stresses the great joy around the births of John the Baptist and Jesus. The angel promised Zechariah joy. Gladness and rejoicing are repeated at the birth of his son (1:14, 58). The baby John "leaps for joy" in Elizabeth's womb (1:41–44). Mary's song of praise begins with "my spirit rejoices" (1:47). Joy issues into praise for Zechariah (1:68–80), Simeon (2:29–32), and Anna (2:38). Jesus' birth is "good news of great joy" (2:10). The angels and the shepherds both respond by "praising God" (2:13, 20).

Joy is connected with food, which Luke seems to have a strong interest in. The prominent "food motif" is found not only in the Gospel but also in Acts. Luke mentions nineteen meals, thirteen of which are peculiar to his Gospel. Jesus is frequently portrayed as being present at meals (5:29; 7:36; 14:1; 22:14; 24:30), and he is criticized for eating too much ("a glutton and a drunkard" [7:34; see 5:33]) and for eating with the wrong people (tax collectors and sinners [5:30; 15:1–2]). Banquets also figure prominently in his parables and teaching as he offers what on the surface appear to be instructions in social etiquette (7:44–46; 12:35–37; 14:7–24; 22:26–27). What might be the purpose of such a theme? In a general sense, meals are often depicted as occasions for healing (9:11–17), hospitality (10:5–7), fellowship (13:29), forgiveness (7:36–50), prophetic teaching (11:37–54), and reconciliation (15:23; 24:30–35). Many biblical scholars note that in Luke, Jesus is either going to or coming from a party. Christians in the early Church met regularly for meals (Acts 2:42, 46).

Joy is also connected with the theme of salvation. Those who encounter Jesus are saved. Three examples: salvation comes to Zacchaeus's house (Luke 19:9), the Son of Man came to seek and to save the lost (19:10), and a thief finds paradise (23:42–43).

The Gospel of Luke could be called the Gospel of Joy, especially for the excluded and outcasts of society:

Samaritans (9:51–56; 10:29–37; 17:11–19)

Gentiles (2:32; 3:23–38; 4:24–27; 7:1–10; 24:47)

Tax collectors (3:12; 5:27–32; 7:34; 15:1–2; 18:9–14; 19:1–10)

Women (1:26–56; 2:36–38; 7:11–17, 36–50; 8:2, 42–48; 10:38–42; 21:1–4; 23:27–31; 23:55—24:11)

The poor (1:53; 4:18; 6:20; 7:22; 14:13, 21; 16:20, 22; 19:8; 21:2–3)

The rich (1:53; 6:24; 12:16–21; 16:1–9, 19–31; 19:1–10)

Finally, for Luke, joy is the fruit of the Holy Spirit. Those who are filled with the Spirit experience joy and wonder. Just as Jesus received the Holy Spirit, the disciples, too, would be filled with the Spirit from on high. According to Luke, God gives the Holy Spirit to all who ask (11:13).

Points for Reflection

- After having heard Peter's speech at Pentecost, the crowds asked, "Brothers, what should we do?" What should you do to receive the gifts of the Holy Spirit?

- Peter was bold and faithful in his testimony. How is God inviting you to be a witness right now? How might you be more bold and faithful?

- Paul writes to the Galatians, saying, "The fruit of the Spirit is love, joy, peace, patience, kindness, generosity, faithfulness, gentleness, self-control. Against such there is no law" (5:22–23). What are some of the fruits of the Holy Spirit that you need at this time in your life?

- What brings you joy? How do you keep your sense of humor?

The Church's *Koinonia*

When Luke sat down to write Acts, years had already passed since those early days of the Church. In the intervening years, the Church had its fair share of ups and downs. One of the most constant issues and conflicts it faced was community life. What does it mean to live together as a community of believers who are ethnically diverse? For Luke, the resurrection of Jesus completely changed things. Believers could no longer live as before but must begin to live and act in a whole new way. They must think differently about their cultural differences, ethnicity, possessions, security, and money. Perhaps as a way to deal with various conflicts in the community, Luke needed to paint an ideal picture of the earliest community to show that, with the gift of the Holy Spirit given at Pentecost, a community can and must become one in mind and soul. They must live in unity despite being ethnically diverse. Let us now see how Luke looks back to "the good old days," but first, pause to read Acts 2:43–47:

> Awe came upon everyone, and many wonders and signs were done through the apostles. All who believed were together and had all things in common; they would sell their property and possessions and divide them among all according to each one's need. Every day they devoted themselves to meeting together in the temple area and to breaking bread in their homes. They ate their meals with exultation and sincerity of heart, praising God and enjoying favor with all the people. And every day the Lord added to their number those who were being saved. (See also 4:32–37; 5:1–11.)

John Mark, the Reconciler

I, Luke, have investigated the earliest community extensively. Everyone I talked to spoke with great fondness. They referred to it as "the good old days." The fruits of the Holy Spirit had led the community to live in a spirit of fellowship, or *koinonia,* as they often named it. One notable interview I had was with a man named John, whose other name was Mark (Acts 12:12, 25). Since Mark happened to pass through Antioch to visit our community while I was gathering information for my second volume, I took the opportunity to sit down and ask him a few questions about "the good old days." Here is an excerpt of the interview.

Luke: "Could you start by telling us a little about yourself?"

Mark: "My name is John Mark, but most people simply call me Mark. I was born in Cyprus, but my family, like many faithful diaspora Jews, immigrated back to Jerusalem to be closer to God and the Temple when I was a child. Everything changed when we met Jesus from Nazareth. Before the destruction of the Temple by the Romans in 70 and before finally settling in Rome, my family used to have a house on Mount Zion, near the Old City, where Jesus and his disciples celebrated their Last Supper. It was also in the same upper room that the first Pentecost took place. My good and pious mother, who is now at peace in heaven with the Lord, I am sure, was Mary. Mom used to have a maid named Rhoda (12:12–13). Rhoda and I have become good friends over the years. I am actually staying at her house in Antioch. I think you have met her already. Recalling all these things really makes me feel nostalgic."

Luke: "I was told that you were in Jerusalem when the earliest *ekklesia* (assembly, congregation, church) was founded. Do you recall what happened? What was it like?"

Mark: "It was an amazing period of the Church! All those who had received the gift of the Holy Spirit were of one heart and

soul. We came from different backgrounds and spoke
different dialects, but we
were completely one. We
even held all our possessions
in common, sold them, and
then distributed the pro-
ceeds according to each person's need. In the beginning,
we would go to the Temple to
pray and then break bread at
home. We were all filled with
gladness and joy. People were
impressed with our commu-
nity spirit. We shared everything in common, which is
called *koinonia*. There was
no needy person among us.
We really took care of one
another. It did not matter
whether you were a man
or a woman, slave or free,
Hebrew or Hellenist Jew.
By the testimony of our *koinonia*, the number of those
who were saved consistently
increased day by day."

Luke: "It sounds like the
nascent *ekklesia* was quite
awesome. But realistically,
was everyone so united and
generous? Were there no
tensions or conflicts?"

**Sidebar 4.1
Biblical Characters**

Who is...*John Mark*?

❖ This person has two names.
John was his Jewish name, and
Mark (Marcus) his Roman name.
Luke tells us that he is "John
who is called Mark" (Acts 12:12).

❖ He was the son of Mary, a
prominent Christian woman
who has a house in Jerusalem.
Mark's mother's house was
apparently a popular place for
Christians, where "many people
gathered in prayer" (Acts 12:12).
It was the first place that the
Apostle Peter sought for refuge
after escaping from prison (Acts
12:6–12). This house could very
well be the upper room where
the Last Supper and Pentecost
took place.

❖ John Mark was a cousin of
Barnabas (Col 4:10). He accompanied Paul and Barnabas on
their first missionary journey.
Although Mark had sharp
disagreement with Paul, he
later became Paul's great
helper and faithful companion
during Paul's imprisonment at
Rome (Col 4:10; Phlm 24). He
was loved by Peter since Peter
referred to him as "my son" (1 Pt
5:13).

❖ He is probably the evangelist
who wrote the earliest Gospel,
namely Mark, which bears his
name.

❖ The Church celebrates his feast
day on April 25.

Mark: "As human beings, we have flaws and weaknesses. Since the Church is made up of people, it was, is, and will be imperfect. That is a fact we must accept, and we should continue to pray for all its members. Returning to the earliest community, there was a couple named Ananias and Sapphira. They were new converts to the faith. They, too, sold a piece of property but only gave a small portion of the proceeds to the *ekklesia*. They were interested in the *koinonia* only for their own interests. They took advantage of the community's generosity. They thought they could deceive God and the apostles. When the community discovered they had kept back part of the money for themselves, the community confronted them, but they persisted in their lies and scheming. One day, however, the couple was found dead in their home from an unknown cause. Some suspected it had something to do with their business scheme. Others in the community believed it was a direct punishment from God. No one knows for sure."

Luke: "In contrast to Ananias and Sapphira, Barnabas was different, for he was quite a generous man. Since you seem to know him quite well, could you tell me a little about him?"

Mark: "Cousin Barni, as I always call him, was one of the first disciples who voluntarily sold all his possessions and laid the proceeds at the apostles' feet. As you already know, Barnabas is my cousin. His real name was Joseph, but when he became a believer, the apostles named him Barnabas, which means "son of encouragement" (Acts 4:36). Barnabas was a Levite who came from my own village in Cyprus. He was generous and a model of discipleship. I cannot say enough about how my cousin Barni was a source of inspiration and support for me and for many others over the years.

"Besides being incredibly generous with his resources, Barnabas was an extraordinary leader and missionary. He saw gifts in others that people normally overlooked. When the church in Jerusalem heard about the conversions in Antioch, Barnabas was sent here to encourage the community. His good nature and holiness won a great number of people to the Lord (11:24). When Paul was still Saul, it was cousin Barni who reached out to Paul and accepted him when others were afraid of him and doubted his conversion.

"In the beginning, Barnabas and Paul were very compatible. They built up the church in Antioch. It was here in Antioch that the believers were first called 'Christians' (11:26). It was from here that Barnabas and Paul were sent on their first missionary journey, taking me along as their helper (13:5). It was actually cousin Barni who first asked me to come to Antioch when he and Paul first visited the Jerusalem church (12:25). Barnabas saw things in me that neither I nor others no-

---

**Sidebar 4.2
Biblical Backgrounds**

What is...*koinonia*?

❖ *Koinonia* is the transliteration of a Greek word that has such a multitude of meanings that no single English word is adequate to express its depth and richness. The best terms that might convey its meaning and significance are communion, fellowship, and community.

❖ The first usage of *koinonia* in the Greek New Testament is found in Acts 2:42–47, where we read a striking description of the common life shared by the early Christian believers in Jerusalem: "They devoted themselves to the teaching of the apostles and to the communal life, to the breaking of the bread and to the prayers...All who believed were together and had all things in common; they would sell their property and possessions and divide them among all according to each one's need...They ate their meals with exultation and sincerity of heart, praising God and enjoying favor with all the people."

❖ Paul also talked about this idealized state of fellowship and community that should exist among Christians (1 Cor 10:16, 11:24–26).

ticed. He encouraged and supported me in times of doubt and trials. During the first missionary journey I grew impatient and abandoned the mission to return to Jerusalem (13:13). Nevertheless, Barnabas gave me another chance to go on a second missionary journey, but unfortunately, Paul refused to take me along because I had deserted them (15:37–40). Cousin Barni stood beside me and supported me throughout that painful ordeal. He even sacrificed his own desire to stay with Paul to go with me to Cyprus to assist me in my mission.

"Looking back now makes me feel really sad. Due to my immaturity and uncompromising spirit, I caused friction between Barnabas and Paul. It could have jeopardized the whole Christian mission. Despite the unfortunate incident, the Spirit gave us the grace to move forward and even expand the mission. I eventually ended up in Rome, where I became a close assistant to the great apostle and pillar of the Church, Peter (1 Peter 5:13). Just recently I also composed the first Gospel of our Lord Jesus Christ, the Son of God (Mark 1:1). As I look back, I cannot help but give thanks to God for giving me cousin Barni, who stood by me in good times as well as in bad times and encouraged me along the way."

Luke: "I'm curious to know what happened between you and Paul. Did you two ever reconcile?"

Mark: "It was very difficult in the beginning. We both had our differences in character as well as perspectives about mission. But we were basically preaching the same Good News of our Lord Jesus Christ, who is Lord and Savior. Jesus taught us to love and to forgive. When Paul and I eventually met again in Rome, we worked out our differences and became co-workers in the vineyard of the Lord (Philemon 24). I actually spent many days and nights assisting and encouraging Paul during his imprisonment" (2 Timothy 4:11; Colossians 4:10).

Forgiveness As Hallmark of Christian Love

When the first missionaries from France came to Alberta, Canada, they were savagely opposed by a young chief of the Cree Indians named Maskepetoon. But he eventually responded to the gospel and accepted Christ. Shortly afterward, a member of the Blackfoot tribe killed Maskepetoon's father. Maskepetoon rode into the village where the murderer lived and demanded that he be brought before him. Confronting the guilty man, he said, "You have killed my father, so now you must be my father. You shall ride my best horse and wear my best clothes." In utter amazement and remorse, his enemy exclaimed, "My son, now you have killed me!" He meant, of course, that the hate in his own heart had been completely erased by the forgiveness and kindness of the Indian chief. [8]

William A. Ward says, "Forgiveness is a funny thing; it warms the heart and cools the sting." Forgiveness is a hallmark of Christian virtue and love. If the gospels are insistent about anything, it is the necessity for forgiveness. Jesus says to his disciples, "If you forgive others their transgressions, your heavenly Father will forgive you. But if you do not forgive others, neither will your Father forgive your transgressions" (Matthew 6:14–15). On another occasion, Jesus told the disciples, "Be merciful, just as your Father is merciful…Forgive and you will be forgiven" (Luke 6:36–37).

Jesus linked the forgiveness of others with the worship of God. He told his followers that if they went to the Temple to pray and remembered a grudge they were holding against someone, they should leave their gift at the altar and go be reconciled first (Matthew 5:23). The implication is, reconciliation is a prerequisite for worshiping God. Or perhaps the implication goes even further: forgiveness is a form of worship.

....

[8] See sermonillustrations.com/a-z/f/forgiveness.htm (accessed May 1, 2013).

So unheard of was this emphasis on forgiveness in Jesus' day that his disciples were very disconcerted by his repeated insistence on it. Among themselves, they murmured, "He can't be serious, can he? There are limits to forgiveness, aren't there?" One day Peter got the courage to ask Jesus about forgiveness in an attempt to establish some sort of reasonable guidelines or logical limits. Peter asked him, "Lord, if my brother sins against me, how often must I forgive him? As many as seven times?" Peter thought he was being generous. But Jesus answered, "Not seven times but seventy-seven times" (Matthew 18:21–22). In other words, there are no limits on how many times we are to forgive. It is easy to imagine how shocked the disciples were by these words, for many of us today continue to be shocked by them.

Jesus did more than preach forgiveness, however. He practiced it—most notably on Calvary and after the resurrection. As he hung dying on the cross, Jesus prayed for his persecutors with the words, "Father, forgive them, they know not what they do" (Luke 23:34). Moreover, after the resurrection, Jesus forgave the disciples who deserted him in his final hours. Unless we, too, forgive as Jesus did, we cannot be his disciples.

The theme "forgiveness of sins," which is synonymous with salvation, is repeated throughout Luke and Acts. In Luke, Zechariah prays for it (1:77), John the Baptist announces it (3:3), Jesus has the authority to absolve it (7:48), the disciples are to preach it (24:47), and in Acts it is announced to those in need of it (2:38; 5:31; 10:43; 13:38; 26:18). The Parable of the Prodigal Son (Luke 15:11–32) is a model of what it means to truly forgive. In the parable, the father eagerly restores the dignity of the son who humbly returns to him. Thus, those who come to Jesus with a repentant heart will also be forgiven. The whole of Jesus' ministry is to bring unprecedented forgiveness of sins (Luke 4:18–21). He does it in his exorcisms, healing, and teaching. When one closely examines the theme of forgiveness of sins in Luke-Acts, one important feature stands out: Forgiveness is strictly God's initiative and gift. It is God who does most of the forgiving (Luke 1:76–77; 5:17–26; 24:45–48; Acts 10:43; 26:17–18), and God offers it without restriction or discrimination. The only thing asked of us is that we are to forgive, just as God has forgiven us.

Thomas A. Edison was working on a crazy contraption called a light bulb, and it took a whole team of men twenty-four hours straight to put just one together. The story goes that when Edison was finished with one light bulb, he gave it to a young boy helper, who nervously carried it up the stairs. Step by step he cautiously watched his hands, obviously frightened of dropping such a priceless piece of work. By now, you've probably guessed what happened; the poor young fellow dropped the bulb at the top of the stairs. It took the entire team of men another twenty-four hours to make another bulb. Finally, tired and ready for a break, Edison was ready to have his bulb carried up the stairs. He gave it to the same young boy who had dropped the first one.[9]

That's true forgiveness. Certainly, forgiveness is never easy, for it goes against our natural instincts. Doris Donnelly, a theologian from Princeton Theological Union, expressed this well when she said, "Forgiveness isn't an instinctive response when we're hurt. When we're hurt, the instinctive response is to fight back, to retaliate, to plan revenge, to do something to get even." [10] Because forgiveness is so difficult, it often takes time and requires a lot of energy. Furthermore, since forgiveness is not instinctive, it has to be learned. Forgiveness is a gift that frees us. It heals relationships and mends our hurts and wounds. Forgiveness is a

....

[9] From bible.org/illustration/thomas-edison-0 (accessed May 1, 2013).

[10] From an interview on Christopher Closeup cited in the Gainesville Sunday (Apr 21, 1984). See news.google.com/newspapers?nid=1320&dat=19840421&id=sTxWAAAAIBAJ&sjid=qOkDAAAAIBAJ&pg=5744,1375255 (accessed May 1, 2013).

powerful force that we must all practice. Let us therefore observe Saint Paul's advice: "Put on then, as God's chosen ones, holy and beloved, heartfelt compassion, kindness, humility, gentleness, and patience, bearing with one another and forgiving one another, if one has a grievance against another; as the Lord has forgiven you, so must you also do" (Colossians 3:12–13).

Points for Reflection

- The early Church was of one heart and soul. The disciples shared everything in common and were fervent in their prayers. They looked out for everyone's needs. What is your attitude about personal possessions and communal prayers? Are you a gift or a burden to the community? How can you become more generous and holy?

- With Barnabas's encouragement, John Mark regained his missionary zeal and Paul's respect. How are you like Barnabas, "a son of encouragement"? Are you willing to help others and patiently work with them even when others reject them? Will you make personal sacrifices to encourage others along the way?

- John Mark's initial failure was not the end of his usefulness to God's kingdom and mission. Barnabas was willing to invest in John Mark even after his failure. Our failures do not need to be the end for us either. Jesus Christ offers us forgiveness and gives each of us the chance for a fresh start. As you experience spiritual renewal at this time in your life, pray that you have a generous heart to always encourage others along the way.

- Have you ever had the experience of forgiving someone who has hurt or wronged you? If so, what helped you to forgive? If not, what prevents you from forgiving?

The Gentile Pentecost

The mission to the gentiles and their integration into the Church were no small matter for the early Christians. Since Jewish purity laws prohibited personal contact with gentiles, Jewish Christians were not allowed to interact and have table fellowship with them. The strict observance of the Mosaic law was clearly an obstacle to the expansion of the Church in general and to the mission to the gentiles in particular. To help resolve a crisis that could have divided the Church, Luke masterfully recounts the story of Peter and Cornelius in a very artistic and dramatic way. This watershed story in Acts of the Apostles, which is the longest narrative found in the New Testament, is often referred to as "the gentile Pentecost" (10:1—11:18). The whole thrust of the story shows that the gentile mission was a fulfillment of God's salvific will and plan for the Church, since it was fully initiated and completely guided by the Holy Spirit. This is a significant turning point for the Church and its mission.[11]

To appreciate the drama as well as the plot of the story, Cornelius—a gentile Roman soldier—will recount his religious and Pentecost experience. His retelling of the event will teach us to always be open to change, which is a trait of healthy spirituality. But first, let us pause to read the Scripture text from Acts 11:1–18:

....

[11] vanThanh Nguyen, *Peter and Cornelius: A Story of Conversion and Mission* (Eugene, OR: Pickwick, 2012).

Now the apostles and the brothers who were in Judea heard that the gentiles too had accepted the word of God. So when Peter went up to Jerusalem the circumcised believers confronted him, saying, "You entered the house of uncircumcised people and ate with them." Peter began and explained it to them step by step, saying, "I was at prayer in the city of Joppa when in a trance I had a vision, something resembling a large sheet coming down, lowered from the sky by its four corners, and it came to me. Looking intently into it, I observed and saw the four-legged animals of the earth, the wild beasts, the reptiles, and the birds of the sky. I also heard a voice say to me, 'Get up, Peter. Slaughter and eat.' But I said, 'Certainly not, sir, because nothing profane or unclean has ever entered my mouth.' But a second time a voice from heaven answered, 'What God has made clean, you are not to call profane.' This happened three times, and then everything was drawn up again into the sky. Just then three men appeared at the house where we were, who had been sent to me from Caesarea. The Spirit told me to accompany them without discriminating. These six brothers also went with me, and we entered the man's house. He related to us how he had seen [the] angel standing in his house, saying, 'Send someone to Joppa and summon Simon, who is called Peter, who will speak words to you by which you and all your household will be saved.' As I began to speak, the holy Spirit fell upon them as it had upon us at the beginning, and I remembered the word of the Lord, how he had said, 'John baptized with water but you will be baptized with the holy Spirit.' If then God gave them the same gift he gave to us when we came to believe in the Lord Jesus Christ, who was I to be able to hinder God?" When they heard this, they stopped objecting and glorified God, saying, "God has then granted life-giving repentance to the gentiles too."

Cornelius, the Faith-Seeker

It was the most life-changing event of my life! Those who have had a religious experience that is similar to my Pentecost experience can attest that such an occurrence is forever etched in one's memory. My experience was both frightening and awe-inspiring. At the same time it was transforming. It all started with a divine vision or "theophany." While I was praying in my house, a man dressed in dazzling robes appeared to me, calling out my name. Even for a veteran soldier and a centurion—commander of a hundred men—like me who was used to giving orders, I was frightened out of my wits, since nothing like this had ever happened to me or to anyone I know. I was certain my eyes had deceived me, so I looked more intently at the bright angelic figure standing in front of me to make sure I was not being delusional. Somehow I mustered

Sidebar 5.1
Biblical Characters

Who is...*Cornelius*?

❖ Cornelius is a Roman centurion based in Caesarea Maritima with a hundred men under his command. He is commonly known as Cornelius the Centurion.

❖ Acts 10:1–8 paints a very positive picture of the man. As a high-ranking military officer, he has a high social status in society. But as a gentile, he is both pious and charitable. He seems to have been a patron of the Jewish community and synagogue in Caesarea.

❖ He belongs to a group called, "God-fearers." While not fully a proselyte, he favors Judaism and monotheism.

❖ According to the chronology of Acts, the conversion of Cornelius occurred before the death of Herod Agrippa in 41.

❖ The story of his conversion was a decisive moment for the expansion of the mission to the gentiles. It set the stage for Paul to go to the ends of the earth.

enough courage to ask, "What is it, sir?" It was really a silly question, but being dumbfounded, it was all I could think to say, because I sincerely wished to know what this man in dazzling robes wanted with me. However, the transcendent figure didn't seem offended by my simple question. Rather, he complimented me, saying, "Your prayers and almsgiving have ascended as a memorial offering before God." I didn't completely understand what he meant, but I think he said my prayers had been heard. I had been praying for the arrival of salvation by God. Like many of my Jewish friends, I longed for the coming of the Messiah. They told me that when Christ comes, he would offer repentance and salvation to anyone who believes in him. I had been longing for that day.

Many of my Roman friends could not understand me. They actually thought I was strange and eccentric in my belief. Unlike them, I was attracted to the worship of one God. Since the worshiping of multiple gods was a common practice for most gentiles, monotheism was seen as peculiar and anomalous. Despite their criticism, I was attracted to monotheism and sought to know and worship the one true God. This is the reason people jeered at me as the foolish "faith-seeker" or "God-fearer." Actually, many people are like me; unfortunately, many of them are secretive about their belief for fear of being ridiculed or ostracized. I, on the other hand, was quite open about my religious preference. I admired the faith of the Jewish people and therefore frequented their synagogue. Although I never became a full member or a proselyte who was required to perform the ritual of circumcision, I supported their faith and even gave generous alms to help construct their synagogue.

When the man in dazzling clothes appeared to me, my life began to take a different path. He commanded me to send men to Joppa and summon a certain Simon, who was also called Peter. He would reveal to me everything about the Christ. The man in the vision even told me that Peter was staying in the house of Simon, a tanner, who lived near the sea. The detail concerning the whereabouts of Peter was helpful, but a curious thought actually crossed my mind as to why he was staying in a tanner's house. Since tanners work with the hides of dead animals, they are considered unclean by most Jews. If this Peter was willing to associate with such a person, I wondered if he might be more open to venturing into a gentile city and a gentile's house. At any rate, the man in the vision provided helpful directions. Although I was not used to being told what to do, I gladly obeyed his command. I immediately called two of my trusted servants and a devout soldier, told them what had happened, and then sent them to Joppa at once. Their mission was to find Peter and persuade him to come to Caesarea as soon as possible.

The distance from Caesarea, or more accurately Caesarea Maritima ("Caesarea by the Sea"), to the ancient seaport of Joppa is about thirty miles, or fifty kilometers. A healthy person could make the journey in a day on foot, but on horses, it is much quicker. For three days I waited with much anxiety. I nervously walked around my house as if I had seen a ghost. I kept reviewing the scene of the man in dazzling robes. *Who was he?* I had no doubt the vision was real. Convincing others, however, would be another matter. My whole

---

**Sidebar 5.2
Biblical Backgrounds**

What is...*circumcision?*

❖ Circumcision is the removal of the foreskin from the male penis and was routinely performed on infants of eight days (Gn 17:12; Lv 12:3; Lk 1:59 and 2:21).

❖ It served as a "sign" of God's covenant with Israel and was the most distinguishing mark separating the Israelites from surrounding peoples. It was a requirement of God's covenant (Gn 17:9–14), along with Sabbath observance and food laws.

❖ It was the most significant marker that distinguished Jew from gentile, those within the covenant from those outside.

❖ In the New Testament, the issue of the requirement of circumcision for gentile Christians gave rise to the Council of Jerusalem (Acts 15:1–29; Gal 2:1–10). At the Council, Peter and Paul insisted that circumcision was not required for gentile Christians, and the church agreed.

household saw something different about me, but they did not know the reason. I couldn't reveal it to them, of course. They would probably think I'd gone mad. Besides the servants whom I sent to Caesarea, I only told my beloved wife. She understood and comforted me greatly.

When I am preoccupied with pressing issues, I often walk along the wharf to ease my troubles. The impressive harbor, built by Herod the Great, was a real feat of engineering. How Herod's engineers were able to create massive concrete slabs and plant them underwater to stop the strong currents from surging over its dikes is still a marvel for many people even today. At the entrance of the harbor stood a giant lighthouse, with fire constantly burning to guide ships safely. One could see the light from many miles away. The seaport brought in many ships from all over the Mediterranean Sea. It gave life and prosperity to the city and to the whole region.

The sea breeze here is always refreshing, and the view of this modern Greco-Roman city is simply breathtaking. From the harbor, one could see the splendid temple of Augustus, built by Herod in honor of his patron, Augustus Caesar. As a matter of fact, the name of this city, Caesarea, is also named in honor of his friend the emperor. The city was the military and administrative capital and the seat of the Roman prefect and governor of the province of Judea. It had a huge hippodrome, a splendid theater, and many bath houses. I was lucky to live in Caesarea, for there was plenty of space to walk around the city and along the waterfront. Usually the view and the cool breeze would ease my tension, but not on those days while I anxiously waited for the arrival of a man whose name means Rock.

On the fourth day news finally arrived that Peter and six other companions were approaching the city. When Peter came near my house, I went out to meet him. After seeing the man, I knelt down to pay him homage, for he exuded much holiness and kindness. But he humbly raised me up and said that he was just an instrument of God. When Peter entered the house and saw that my household had also been assembled, he was impressed and said, "You know that it is unlawful for a Jewish man to associate with, or visit, a gentile, but God has shown me that I should not call any person profane or unclean. And that is why I came without objection when sent for. May I ask, then, why you summoned me?"

And so I recounted what I had seen and heard in the vision. I specifically said that it was the Lord who had commanded me to summon him here to reveal to everyone who the Christ was. Thus Peter began to tell us about Jesus Christ, who is Lord of all, and what had happened all over Judea, beginning in Galilee after the baptism that John preached, how God anointed Jesus of Nazareth with the Holy Spirit and power. He went about doing good and healing all those oppressed by the devil. However, the leaders in Jerusalem crucified him, but God raised him on the third day and he appeared to many. Some even ate and drank with him after he rose from the dead. He then commissioned the apostles to preach the Good News and testify that he is the one appointed by God as judge of the living and the dead. To him, all the prophets bore witness that everyone who believes in him will receive forgiveness of sins through his name.

While Peter was still speaking, I suddenly realized that I, too, have seen the Lord. The man in dazzling robes who appeared to me four days ago was none other than Jesus Christ, the risen Lord! At that very moment I came to believe everything. And then I felt a sudden rush of wind and fire pouring out over me and my whole household. We began to speak in tongues and glorify God in languages that everyone could understand. Peter and his six companions were utterly shocked, for the Holy Spirit had been poured out even upon us gentiles, just as had happened at Pentecost in the upper room in Jerusalem.

Openness to Change As Healthy Spirituality

John Cardinal Newman once said, "To live is to change, and to be perfect is to have changed often." Change is inevitable and a fact of life. The whole cosmos is constantly in flux, moving and shifting. Nature changes and so do the seasons. Our skin, hair, teeth, and organs are continually evolving and developing. The Buddha said, "Change is the only consistent thing in life." Change is ever-present, so why do we resist it? Because it causes stress! No one likes change. We're used to routines and prefer the same old, same old, even when we know it's harmful. We cave in to change because old habits always seem to creep back in and defeat our motivation and willpower. A proverb says, "Some people will change when they see the light. Others change only when they feel the heat." What about you? How do you react to change? Since spirituality is connected with a willingness to change, an openness to change is another essential characteristic for nurturing a healthy spirituality.

However, the change I speak of here is not just something casual for the sake of change, like many New Year resolutions that are soon forgotten. Rather, it is conversion, or *metanoi*, in the service of the mission of Jesus Christ and in a daily commitment to live the Gospel values. It is a personal response to Jesus' invitation to "follow him" and to the eschatological urgency to "repent and believe in the Good News."

For conversion to take place, one must be open to hear God's word. Throughout Acts of the Apostles, Luke consistently shows that salvation is offered to those who are willing to hear the word preached to them (2:37; 4:4; 8:6; 13:44, 48; 18:8; 19:5, 10). Apart from hearing the word, salvation is not really possible (17:32). Cornelius is a good example of someone who is open to hear and be changed. Although a gentile, Cornelius is depicted like a pious Jew who is "devout," "gives alms generously," and "prays to God constantly" (10:2). Furthermore, the reader is told twice (by Cornelius's messengers and by Cornelius himself) about his desire "to hear" all that Peter has to say (10:22) and all that has been commanded by the Lord (10:33). The narrator also recounts that Cornelius was anxiously awaiting the arrival of Peter (10:24b). When Peter arrived, Cornelius told the apostle what the man in dazzling robes had revealed to him, "Cornelius, your prayer has been heard…" (10:31). It is not certain what that prayer entailed; however from the context of the dialogue, it is very possible that his prayer had to do with his desire to hear the message of salvation. Being a God-fearer and a faith-seeker, Cornelius would certainly want to be enlightened by the truth. Thus, the command to summon a certain Peter from Joppa to speak words by which he and his household would be saved was exactly what Cornelius needed and longed for.

Cornelius's receptivity of God's word led him to repentance and conversion. Luke tells us that "the holy Spirit fell upon all who were listening to the word" (Acts 10:44) and that "the gentiles too had accepted the word of God" (11:1). The Jerusalem community confirms that "God has then granted life-giving repentance to the gentiles too" (11:18). According to Luke, therefore, Cornelius's receptivity of God's word led him to *metanoia*. His response is paradigmatic, not only for God-fearers or gentile converts, but for all believers.

Peter, the Rock, did not remain unchanged in his behavior and theology. As a strict observer of the Mosaic Law and one who never eats "anything profane and unclean" (10:14), Peter was open to the guidance of the Holy Spirit. Though Peter was hesitant to venture into gentile territory and enter a gentile home, he was willing to take chances. Consequently, having witnessed the Spirit's descending upon Cornelius and his household in the same way that he himself had experienced at Pentecost, Peter without question and without hesitation ordered the gentiles to be baptized immediately and then dined with them without qualms (10:47–48; 11:3).

Peter's action and behavior demonstrate a deep conversion of heart and theology. He perceives God as "impartial," showing no favoritism toward anyone or any nation in particular. As long as a person fears the Lord and does what is right, that person is acceptable to God. Peter used this theology to convince his opponents in Jerusalem to accept the gentile mission. In the defense, Peter explained to the Jerusalem assembly that the whole Cornelius episode was initiated and directed by God. According to Peter, it was God who showed him the "vision of the cloth" and told him "to slaughter and eat." It was God who told him to go to Caesarea without discrimination. It was God who had commanded Cornelius to summon him to his house. And more important, it was God who poured out the same gift of the Holy Spirit upon the gentiles. Peter was just an instrument responding to divine promptings.

The Christian community in Jerusalem was not in perfect harmony about the issue of gentile membership in the Church. There was clearly dissension over Peter's having gone to the home of the uncircumcised and having participated in table fellowship with them. Peter clearly had broken the Church's rules and regulations. This issue was no small matter. But through dialogue and communal discernment, the Jerusalem church eventually became convinced that it was God's will that the gentiles be included in the Christian community and that table fellowship with them was acceptable. Noticeably, the Church began with fierce resistance but ended by glorifying God, saying, "God has granted even to the gentiles the repentance unto life."

The theme of conversion dominates a good portion of the Acts of the Apostles. The first story of mass conversion happened at Pentecost. Through Peter's inspired sermon, three thousand people came to believe in Jesus Christ. Through Philip's proclamation, many people in Samaria repented and turned to Christ (8:5–15). Philip also assisted the Ethiopian eunuch to understand the Hebrew Scriptures and to be baptized in the name of Jesus Christ (8:26–38). There is the famous conversion of Saul or Paul, which is so important that Luke relates Paul's experience three times: 9:1–18; 22:6–16; 26:12–18. The episode of Peter and Cornelius along with his household is the watershed story of the gentile mission (10:1—11:18). Many other people were converted through the preaching of the apostles: the Proconsul and other gentiles (Acts 13); Lydia and the jailer (Acts 16); Dionysius, Damaris, and a few others (Acts 17); Crispus and Apollos (Acts 18); and twelve disciples of John the Baptist (Acts 19) [See 19:7]. Acts of the Apostles narrates numerous conversion stories, inviting readers then and now to foster a spirituality of openness to repentance (*metanoia*) for salvation.

Points for Discussion

- Cornelius, the faith-seeker and God-fearer, had a religious experience that turned his life around and the lives of those close to him. How much has your vocation, as a baptized Christian or a professed religious, influenced the behavior and actions of those around you?

- People go through three possible stages when confronted with change: (1) resistance to change; (2) tolerance of change; or (3) embracing the change. What about you? How do you normally confront change?

- John Cardinal Newman said, "To live is to change. To have lived well is to have changed often." What are some of the changes you have resolved to make? More important, what is God inviting you to change today?

The Jerusalem Council

The early Christian Church was not without upheaval and conflict. One of the main issues the early Church faced was who was welcome and who was not. Due to religious observances and purity codes dictated in the Jewish Torah, gentiles were definitely not welcome, especially at table fellowship! There were some believers and even apostles, for example Paul, who were more lenient with the question of inclusion and exclusion. The issue was no small matter. It could have split the church. Clearly the church has changed since those early days of prohibition and discrimination against gentile believers. How did it happen? How did the early church resolve this critical issue that could have destroyed the church? In this chapter we will hear the words of an eyewitness, namely Barnabas, who will tell his side of the story in a form of a letter. But first, let us pause to read Acts 15:1–20. What does this Scripture passage and story teach us about decision-making and conflict resolution?

> Some who had come down from Judea were instructing the brothers, "Unless you are circumcised according to the Mosaic practice, you cannot be saved." Because there arose no little dissension and debate by Paul and Barnabas with them, it was decided that Paul, Barnabas, and some of the others should go up to Jerusalem to the apostles and presbyters about this question. They were sent on their journey by the church, and passed through Phoenicia and Samaria telling of the conversion of the gentiles, and brought great joy to all the brothers. When they arrived

in Jerusalem, they were welcomed by the church, as well as by the apostles and the presbyters, and they reported what God had done with them. But some from the party of the Pharisees who had become believers stood up and said, "It is necessary to circumcise them and direct them to observe the Mosaic law."

The apostles and the presbyters met together to see about this matter. After much debate had taken place, Peter got up and said to them, "My brothers, you are well aware that from early days God made his choice among you that through my mouth the gentiles would hear the word of the gospel and believe. And God, who knows the heart, bore witness by granting them the holy Spirit just as he did us. He made no distinction between us and them, for by faith he purified their hearts. Why, then, are you now putting God to the test by placing on the shoulders of the disciples a yoke that neither our ancestors nor we have been able to bear? On the contrary, we believe that we are saved through the grace of the Lord Jesus, in the same way as they." The whole assembly fell silent, and they listened while Paul and Barnabas described the signs and wonders God had worked among the gentiles through them.

After they had fallen silent, James responded, "My brothers, listen to me. Symeon has described how God first concerned himself with acquiring from among the gentiles a people for his name. The words of the prophets agree with this, as is written: 'After this I shall return and rebuild the fallen hut of David; from its ruins I shall rebuild it and raise it up again, so that the rest of humanity may seek out the Lord, even all the gentiles on whom my name is invoked. Thus says the Lord who accomplishes these things, known from of old.' It is my judgment, therefore, that we ought to stop troubling the gentiles who turn to God, but tell them by letter to avoid pollution from idols, unlawful marriage, the meat of strangled animals, and blood.

Barnabas, the Encourager

Dear Luke,

Grace and peace to you from our Lord Jesus Christ! I give thanks to God always for you and the ministry you are carrying on at Antioch. Your good works have reached my ears, which made my heart cheerful and my spirit refreshed. I have found much encouragement from your dedication and zeal for the Christian mission. May our Lord grant you wisdom and strength to complete the project entrusted to you, that you will be able to accurately record all the Spirit has done in the Church since the very beginning.

Concerning your request about what actually happened at the Jerusalem Council some years ago, I write this letter with great pleasure to recall one of the most grace-filled moments of the Church in which I was honored to witness and participate. The Jerusalem Council, as you already know, was a significant turning point for the Christian mission. Had the council not taken place,

Sidebar 6.1
Biblical Characters

Who is...*Barnabas*?

❖ He was a Levite and a native of Cyprus, whose real name was Joseph, but the apostles gave him a new name, Barnabas, which means "son of encouragement."

❖ He possessed land, which he sold and then gave the proceeds to the church in Jerusalem (Acts 4:36–37).

❖ He was one of the first teachers of the church at Antioch (Acts 13:1) and a companion of Paul on the first missionary journey. The people in Lystra regarded Paul as Hermes, and Barnabas as Zeus (Acts 14:12).

❖ Barnabas participated in the Council of Jerusalem, and together with Paul, proposed that gentiles be allowed into the community without being circumcised.

❖ True to his name, he gave the young John Mark, his cousin (Col 4:10), a second chance even when it meant having to part company with Paul.

❖ Tertullian, a well-known Christian writer who lived around 160–225, regarded Barnabas as the author of the Letter to the Hebrews.

❖ His feast day falls on June 11. He is a patron against hailstorms and for peacemakers.

our mission to the gentiles would have been difficult or even impossible.

Let me begin by setting the religious and historical contexts that led to the convening of the council. You are aware that many of the first Christians, like myself, came directly from Jewish background and traditions. As faithful Jews, we continued to observe the Old Testament laws that governed all aspects of our daily life. The kind of foods we eat and whom we eat with matters greatly. Even as Christians, we still kept the Mosaic laws.

As the Christian message spread to other towns and villages, gentiles also received the Word and became believers. In some cities, more gentiles than Jews were converted to Christianity. Some gentile converts readily accepted the whole Mosaic Law, but most found some of the teachings in the Torah burdensome and extremely difficult to observe. The older men particularly refused to perform the circumcision ritual. Circumcision had been the sign of the covenant and blessings for the Jewish people from the time of Abraham; thus most Jewish Christians, including myself at first, felt that circumcision was an essential prerequisite for admission and full participation in the Church. Most gentile believers, however, could not understand why they should have to become Jews to become Christians. Furthermore, they could not see a connection between the physical mark of circumcision and their faith in Jesus as Lord and Christ.

The Apostle Paul, who claimed to have been commissioned by the risen Lord to preach to the gentiles, was much more radical in his views than all the other apostles. Having been convinced by Paul's argument and, moreover, having witnessed the faith of the gentile believers on my first missionary journey, I too came to believe that gentile Christians should not be forced to observe the Mosaic Law. This has been our position from that time until now. Unfortunately, not all—even most—Jewish Christians agreed with our radical stance. Some Judaizers—meaning conservative Jewish Christians who claimed that gentile converts must observe the Mosaic Law, particularly circumcision, to be saved—came to Antioch to challenge our practice and even undermine our mission. They tried to discredit Paul's apostleship and his gospel message. The debate was fierce. It caused quite a commotion and dissension in the *ekklesia*. Unable to resolve the crisis, the assembly agreed that it was best to send a delegation to Jerusalem to discuss the issue with the apostles and the elders. Thus Paul and I, along with a few others, went up to Jerusalem to attend the first council of the Church.

Along the way, we met with various Christian communities and reported to everyone about the conversion of the gentiles in foreign territories. The news brought great joy to many believers. It took us many days to reach Jerusalem, but we finally arrived on a spring day in the year 50. James, the brother of the Lord and the leader of the church in

---

Sidebar 6.2
Biblical Backgrounds

What is...*the Jerusalem Council*?

❖ Also known as the Apostolic Conference, it was the earliest Christian gathering of leaders held in Jerusalem and dated to around the year 50.

❖ The reason for the council was that some conservative Christian Jews, who came to Antioch from Judea, obligated gentile converts to be circumcised according to the Mosaic practice. To settle the matter, Paul, Barnabas, and a few others were sent to Jerusalem to speak with the apostles and presbyters.

❖ The council decided that gentile converts to Christianity were not obligated to keep all the Mosaic law, including the rules concerning circumcision of males. The council did, however, retain the prohibitions on eating blood, and meat of animals not properly slain, and on fornication and idolatry.

❖ References to the Jerusalem Council are found in Acts 15 and Galatians 2.

Jerusalem; Peter, also known as Cephas; John and other apostles and elders welcomed us with gladness and joy.

Shortly after our arrival, a small private gathering was assembled. Paul, who was filled with the Holy Spirit, spoke eloquently and persuasively about the will and plan of God that gentiles were turning to the Lord. He described the revelation he had received on the way to Damascus and how the risen Lord appeared to him and commissioned him to preach the Good News to the gentiles, just as Peter was doing for the circumcised. He told the Church about the success they had witnessed among the gentiles in Cilicia and Galatia. He convincingly demonstrated that the Spirit of the Lord was clearly at work in and through them. He even presented to the assembly Titus, an uncircumcised Greek, who came along with us.

At this point in the conference, some false believers who had secretly slipped in raised their voices and protested, saying, "Unless one is circumcised according to the Law of Moses, he cannot be saved!" The debate became increasingly tense. People's voices grew louder.

Just when chaos was about to break loose, Peter stood and intervened. He recalled the event that took place in the house of the gentile Roman centurion named Cornelius. Peter clearly pointed out that the Holy Spirit was poured out upon him and his gentile household just as it did on the day of Pentecost. Peter demonstrated that God made no distinction between Jews and gentiles. To impose circumcision and the observance of the Mosaic Law upon the gentiles would be putting God to the test.

Peter concluded the speech by stating that salvation comes through grace and faith and not through the law. With the words of Peter, the whole assembly fell silent. Thus it was agreed that Paul and I should continue to preach the Good News of Jesus Christ to the uncircumcised, while Peter and others would address the circumcised. No stipulations were imposed upon gentile believers, not even circumcision! The one thing that was asked of us is to remember the poor, which we were very eager to do.[12]

The decision at the Jerusalem Council was monumental. It gave affirmation to our mission and allowed us to participate fully in table fellowship with our gentile brothers and sisters. The Spirit of the Lord was clearly at work among us.

I hope this brief description of the events at the Jerusalem

....

[12] The proposed reconstruction of the event is taken from both Acts 15 and Galatians 2:1–10. Careful readers will notice that these two accounts have various differences and even contain contradictory details. According to Luke, Paul was sent by the church in Antioch (Acts 15:2–3); according to Paul, he went because of a revelation (Galatians 2:2a). In Acts, the gathering was a public meeting (15:12); according to Paul, it was a private one (Galatians 2:2). According to Luke, Paul did not seem to play a major role in the debate; in Galatians, Paul was fierce and was a major player in the discussion and decision-making. What is most strikingly different is that in Acts, a decree was issued concerning the observance of dietary laws and some other moral restrictions; according to Paul, there was no such decree. Nowhere in Paul's letters does this decree or any indication of its existence appear.

Due to the discrepancies and differences in the two accounts, some scholars suggest the possibility that two separate incidents or meetings took place. The first one, which Acts 15:3–12 and Galatians 2:1–10 parallel, dealt exclusively with the issue of circumcision, at which Paul was present and contributed greatly to the debate and outcome of the event. The second event, which is reported in Acts 15:13–33 and seemed to have occurred at a time when Paul was not present, dealt with the issue of dietary laws. Since Paul was not present, he knew nothing about the decree. Fitzmyer distinguishes these two events by calling the first "The Jerusalem Council" and the latter "the Jerusalem Decree." See Joseph A. Fitzmyer, *The Acts of the Apostles* (Anchor Bible; New York: Doubleday, 1998), 543–544; Luke T. Johnson, *The Acts of the Apostles* (Sacra Pagina; Collegeville, MN: Liturgical Press, 1992), 269–270.

Council will assist you in the composition of your writing project. What I have reported is true, for I, Barnabas, write it with my own hand. Finally, my brothers and sisters from the *ekklesia* in Alexandria, Egypt, send you greetings. May the peace of our Lord Jesus Christ and the grace of his Spirit be with you always.

Your Friend in Christ,
Barnabas from Cyprus

Encouragement As Ministry of the Holy Spirit

Life is full of challenges and difficulties. Adversity is a fact of life no one can elude. According to the Buddha, life is suffering. This is Buddhism's first principle of the Four Noble Truths. In his best-selling book, *The Road Less Traveled*, M. Scott Peck begins with the profound truth, "Life is difficult."[13] Sometimes the reality of life—a setback in our goals, the loss of a loved one, or just feeling down or uncertain about the future—can stop us from moving forward and raising our chin.

A healthy spirituality, however, does not deny the fact that life is often arduous and problematic. During these grueling times, some positive words of encouragement can help shift our focus and provide recourse for moving forward. Inspirational words of encouragement from a mentor or a friend can often help us bounce back. When I first entered the seminary, I was a very shy Asian boy. Since I was just a mediocre student, many teachers and even formators[14] questioned my religious vocation. But my spiritual director and mentor, Father Frank,

....

[13] M. Scott Peck, MD, *The Road Less Traveled: A New Psychology of Love, Traditional Values and Spiritual Growth* (25th Anniversary Edition; New York: Simon & Schuster, 1978/2002), 15.

[14] In a religious community, formators function as mentors who help form or guide a younger or newer member of the community.

believed in me and kept encouraging me to study hard and pursue my dreams. He said, "Never be afraid of the unknown to a known God." These words still give me comfort and encouragement.

As I perused the Bible to find inspiration for the theme of encouragement, I stumbled onto the character of Barnabas and became thoroughly fascinated with his personality. Although his original name was Joseph, a Levite from Cyprus, the apostles chose to call him Barnabas, which literally means "son of encouragement" (Acts 4:36). In the Bible, the change of name is far more significant than we might think, for the name of a person often symbolizes the person's character or virtue. Undoubtedly, the apostles observed the character of Joseph and gave him the name Barnabas because it fittingly portrayed his personality. It is noteworthy to point out that the word *encouragement (paraclesis)* is closely connected to the Holy Spirit, who is also known as the "Comforter" or "Advocate" (*paracletos*). Interestingly, these two words are essentially the same in Greek. One of the ministries or works of the Holy Spirit is to encourage us in times of trial and tribulation. Apparently, one of Barnabas's strong qualities was a great capacity to encourage others. Allow me, therefore, to explore what the Scriptures preserved of his behavior to justify the name he was given, namely, Barnabas, the "son of encouragement."

First, he was given the name Barnabas early on when he sold all his property and gave the money to the community so that the proceeds could be shared with anyone in need (Acts 4:37). His action clearly demonstrates his generous character. Furthermore, when we make a sacrifice for common cause and share our wealth with others, that is certainly encouraging to those we join.

The second example is found in Acts 9 where Barnabas reaches out to Paul while others are still suspicious and fearful, for he was known to be a zealous persecutor of the Church. Acts of the Apostles reports that after his dramatic encounter with the Lord on the road to Damascus, Paul eventually came to Jerusalem to meet with the Church leaders. Suspecting that he was a spy, they were afraid of him, "not believing that he was a disciple" (Acts 9:26). This is where Barnabas steps in. He took Paul in and brought him before the apostles. He then reported how Paul had met the risen Christ and had spoken to him, and how Paul had spoken boldly in the name of Jesus (Acts 9:27). Because of the timely support of Barnabas, the disciples in Jerusalem embraced Paul as a fellow minister in the Church.

The third example shows how Barnabas animated the spirit of the newly converted gentiles. It was a remarkable ministry of encouragement. We need to realize that, in the first century, the gentiles were regarded by the Jews as outsiders who were unfit for God's kingdom. When Jewish Christians in Jerusalem heard the report of the gentiles' turning to Christ through the preaching among the scattered Hellenists, they became suspicious of this unapproved activity. Thus the Jerusalem church sent Barnabas to Antioch to investigate. What did Barnabas see and do? Luke succinctly states, "When he arrived and saw the grace of God, he rejoiced and encouraged them all to remain faithful to the Lord in firmness of heart" (Acts 11:23). Barnabas acted with remarkable sensitivity and courage by affirming the authenticity of the gentiles' conversion, and therefore all the gentiles were greatly encouraged and strengthened.

Eventually, Barnabas sought out Paul in Tarsus and brought him to Antioch, where they were sent out on their first missionary journey. They traveled together, preached the Good News of Jesus Christ, and planted new churches in the southern region of Galatia and Asia Minor. Following the success of the first missionary journey, Paul and Barnabas made plans for a second journey. However, this is when the situation became difficult and quarrelsome. Barnabas wanted to take John, who was also called Mark, but Paul obstinately refused because John Mark had deserted them during the first missionary journey (Acts 15:37–38).

We are not told why John Mark dropped out of the first missionary journey. We can only surmise that perhaps the pressures of the missionary endeavors were too much for his physical stamina or too different from what he, who was probably a young lad at the time, had anticipated or envisioned. Whatever the reason, Paul was not going to take another chance with John Mark. Luke reports that Paul and Barnabas had such a sharp disagreement that they parted company (Acts 15:39). Paul decided to take Silas instead, and they went off to Syria and Cilicia. Barnabas, on the other hand, took John Mark and sailed to Cyprus. We do not really know the motivation behind Barnabas's decision to include John Mark. It is possibly because of their family connection since they were cousins (Colossians 4:10). However, given the nature of Barnabas, it might have something to do with his encouraging spirit by giving John Mark another chance to prove himself. We know from history that John Mark did prove himself reliable and trustworthy. He became the first evangelist to record the story of Jesus, eventually reconciled with Paul, and collaborated with Paul until the very end. For more details about John Mark, see chapter 4.

The list of examples is indeed impressive and inspiring. We know that everyone needs encouragement in times of weakness and trial. When Barnabas sold all his property for the common cause, it must have been tremendously encouraging for those who had benefited from his sacrifice and generosity. When Paul was suspected of being a spy, Barnabas alone stood up for Paul and included him in the Church. Barnabas also affirmed the authenticity of the gentiles' conversion in Antioch. It was encouraging also for the young John Mark to be given another chance to prove himself.

When we are doubted and challenged and someone stands by our side as Barnabas did for Paul, for the gentile church, and for John Mark, it is encouraging. Moreover, when someone says,

"I need your help" or "I believe in your gifts," that is reassuring. Barnabas was truly a son of encouragement. He had a gift for it. He gave it freely, even when it cost him dearly. Scripture paints a picture of Barnabas as a kind, forgiving, encouraging, and compassionate man. Luke sums up his character in this way, "He was a good man, filled with the holy Spirit and faith" (Acts 11:24). In the same verse, Luke added that wherever he went, "a large number of people were added to the Lord." Although Barnabas was certainly far from perfect, no more or less than any one of us, he was nevertheless praised for his ministry of lifting up people's spirits. How encouraging for us![15]

Everyone needs a bit of encouragement from time to time. Thankfully we have the Bible as our ultimate source of encouragement. The Bible is the living Word of God and a storehouse of treasures. The following is a list of my favorite Bible verses for encouragement. These verses have lifted my spirit in times of distress and anguish. I pray that these inspiring quotes are as encouraging for you as they have been for me.

"Be strong and steadfast; have no fear or dread of them, for it is the LORD, your God, who marches with you; he will never fail you or forsake you" (Deuteronomy 31:6).

"I command you: be strong and steadfast! Do not fear nor be dismayed, for the LORD, your God, is with you wherever you go" (Joshua 1:9).

"Do not fear: I am with you; do not be anxious: I am your God. I will strengthen you, I will help you, I will uphold you with my victorious right hand" (Isaiah 41:10).

....

[15] I would like to thank Stan Uroda, SVD, for sharing with me his homily on the occasion of the feast of Saint Barnabas. It was his inspiring homily that gave me insights to write this piece about Barnabas. Similar to Saint Barnabas, Stan is a person who always encourages others. I am deeply grateful to Stan for his encouragement and friendship.

"Even though I walk through the valley of the shadow of death, I will fear no evil, for you are with me; your rod and your staff comfort me" (Psalm 23:4).

"Therefore, we are not discouraged; rather, although our outer self is wasting away, our inner self is being renewed day by day" (2 Corinthians 4:16).

"Come to me, all you who labor and are burdened, and I will give you rest. Take my yoke upon you and learn from me, for I am meek and humble of heart; and you will find rest for your selves" (Matthew 11:28–29).

"Have no anxiety at all, but in everything, by prayer and petition, with thanksgiving, make your requests known to God. Then the peace of God that surpasses all understanding will guard your hearts and minds in Christ Jesus" (Philippians 4:6–7).

Being an encouraging person is difficult in a world that often focuses on mistakes and blame. But that is exactly why we, especially young people today, need people like Barnabas—parents, uncles, aunts, spiritual directors, and mentors—who believe in us no matter what, through both the victories and the valleys of life. Finally, we can encourage others by focusing on similarities rather than on differences, just as Barnabas did at the Council of Jerusalem. Allow me to conclude this section with a prayer:

God of infinite love,
you created all peoples in your image.

We thank you for the wonderful diversity of races and cultures in this world.

Look with compassion on the whole human family; take away the arrogance and hatred which infect our hearts; break down the walls that separate us; unite us in bonds of love; and work through our struggle and confusion to accomplish your purposes on earth.

Enrich our lives by ever-widening circles of fellowship, and show us your presence in those who differ most from us.

In life's difficult journey,
may your living words give us comfort and
encouragement to move forward.

When others face failures and setbacks
may we stand by their side and offer words
of encouragement and hope.

Amen.

Points for Reflection

- The early Church resolved conflict and division through dialogue. How important is dialogue in resolving conflict and differences in your family, with your friends, and in your community? What kind of attitude is necessary for good and productive dialogue?

- The early Church leaders had to face many pressing issues and difficult decisions. They did it through communal discernment, prayer, and storytelling. Is there a decision you have to make today? How will you go about making a good decision based on the will of God?

- Who are your prophetic dialogue partners? Will you be more open to other people's ideas, suggestions, and point of view?

- Name some of the people who have encouraged you in times of difficulty. How could you be more encouraging rather than discouraging?

The First European Convert

Our stories continue with Paul and his company being on the road. After a brief rest from the first journey, Paul embarked on a new missionary venture, taking with him Silas and eventually being joined by Timothy and Luke. This journey took them through the northern part of Asia Minor and across the Aegean Sea into Europe. The expedition covered about three thousand miles and lasted about three years. They visited many new cities and founded new communities. It was during the second missionary journey that Paul crossed over into Europe for the first time, not by design, but by the will of the Holy Spirit. During the night Paul had a vision of a Macedonian man imploring, "Come over to Macedonia and help us!"

Recognizing the vision as a sign from God, Paul departed at once into uncharted territory. When he arrived at Philippi, Paul met and converted the first European. Interestingly, it was not a man as seen in the vision but a woman. Her name was Lydia from Thyatira. Exploring the details of her life and conversion will yield a much fuller appreciation for her discipleship and spirituality. Furthermore, through her own narration concerning how she received God's word and message, we may be inspired to imitate the spirit of gratitude and generosity of this early Christian convert. As you read Acts 16:11–15, notice that the encounter between Paul and Lydia is rendered in a rare first-person narration:[16]

....

[16] Biblical scholars call these the "we-passages." See Sidebar 7.2.

We set sail from Troas, making a straight run for Samothrace, and on the next day to Neapolis, and from there to Philippi, a leading city in that district of Macedonia and a Roman colony. We spent some time in that city. On the Sabbath we went outside the city gate along the river where we thought there would be a place of prayer. We sat and spoke with the women who had gathered there. One of them, a woman named Lydia, a dealer in purple cloth, from the city of Thyatira, a worshiper of God, listened, and the Lord opened her heart to pay attention to what Paul was saying. After she and her household had been baptized, she offered us an invitation, "If you consider me a believer in the Lord, come and stay at my home," and she prevailed on us.

Lydia, the Persistent Hostess

It was a good move. Philippi is an important Roman colony on the Via Egnatia, the principal route between Rome and Byzantium. It is located on the eastern border of the Roman province of Macedonia, which is not too far from Thyatira where I used to live. The air is cleaner here, and the scenery is more beautiful. The land is fertile because the area is surrounded by many rivers. The largest river, the Gangites, is found just over a mile from the city center. Situated approximately ten miles inland from the Aegean Sea, with Neapolis as its port, Philippi is known as the gateway into Macedonia. King Philip II, the father of Alexander the Great, captured the city in 356 BCE and renamed it after himself.

I came from Thyatira, which is a city in the province of Lydia located in western Asia Minor. Since I was from that region, my former owner called me Lydia, which is an ethnic designation of my place of origin. That is how I was stuck with that name. I was once a slave and learned the business of manufacturing and producing textiles. I also dealt with purple cloths, for which Thyatira was well known all over the empire. The trade of purple dye was a lucrative industry. The color purple is associated with royalty and luxury. It is the clothing of kings and emperors. Purple is also found in the clothes or togas of the upper-class elites. Purple dye also has other uses in Roman society, such as women's cosmetics, victory marches, and funeral processions. Purple dye is extracted from murex, or seashells, that contain a small bladder holding a tiny amount of juice. This juice is extracted, purified, and manufactured into varying grades of purple dye. It takes about 60,000 murex snails to make one pound of purple dye.

Sidebar 7.1
Biblical Characters

Who is...*Lydia*?

❖ She was a seller of purple cloths who was originally from the city of Thyatira in western Asia Minor. She moved to Philippi and was converted to Christianity by Paul.

❖ She was a "God-fearer," widow, free woman, and patron of the community at Philippi.

❖ She appears only in Acts 16:11–15, 40.

❖ Different churches celebrate her feast day differently. The Latin Rite Catholic Church honors her on August 3.

Consequently, purple dye is rare and very costly, which is why it is primarily used by the elite and the wealthy class.

After years of hard work, my husband and I were eventually able to purchase our freedom. It was a dream come true, for we were no longer slaves but free! With the little money we had left after the manumission, my husband and I, along with our three children, left Thyatira, the place of our enslavement, and emigrated to a new world, hoping for new opportunities.[17] We settled

....

[17] My hypothesis concerning Lydia's marital status is based on Richard Ascough's historical reconstruction. According to Ascough, the most likely scenario is that Lydia was either divorced or most likely widowed, and she probably had at least three or four surviving children living with her. For a more detailed analysis of the social context of Lydia's marital status, see Richard Ascough, *Lydia: Paul's Cosmopolitan Hostess* (Collegeville, MN: Liturgical Press, 2009), 35–45.

in Philippi. Since we were already familiar with manufacturing and producing textiles, especially in purple cloths, we continued in that business. True purple dye was expensive and was under strict imperial control. Thus we decided to produce a cheaper quality of purple that would be more affordable for many people. We started out with a small business, but it grew quickly. Business was extremely good in those early years, for we were the first in this region to manufacture this type of textiles. In just a short period of time, we were able to expand our business and eventually bought a lovely *domus,* a Roman house with an internal garden surrounded by a columned courtyard.[18] Several years later my husband fell ill and died suddenly, leaving me to run the business and our large household by myself.[19]

Although it is difficult to be a female merchant and alone in a man's world, I nevertheless chose to remain a widow. Together with a few other widows, I was able to establish a network of support and business partnerships. I even get together frequently with these women at the riverbank to pray and discuss religious topics. Even though I was a gentile, I always gave thanks to the gods for my blessings. I was drawn particularly to the religious belief of the Jews. I occasionally participated in their worship and joined them in their synagogue. I even supported them financially in their cause. Since I was sympathetic to the Jewish monotheistic

....

[18] A courtyard that has an open garden surrounded by columned porch or open colonnade is called a peristyle. This type of peristyle house was typical in the Roman period. They are found at Pompeii and Ephesus. See Ascough, *Lydia,* 33–34.

[19] A normal Roman household would be comprised not only of immediate family members but also of extended family members (for example, in-laws, grandparents, and cousins) and slaves. See Ascough, *Lydia,* 32–33.

belief, I became known as a "God-fearer."[20] But that was before I met Paul from Tarsus!

On a Sabbath day, while the other God-fearing women and I were gathering along the riverbank to pray, Paul and his traveling companions (Silas, Timothy, and Luke) approached and started to converse with us. At first I was thoroughly shocked by their unusual behavior, for Jewish men do not associate with gentiles, especially gentile women. I have been told on various occasions that women are not appropriate recipients of religious counsel and education. God's word and work are revealed through the Scriptures to men. Women should simply follow what is taught by men and therefore should not question the authority of their teaching. But Paul's attitude toward women was completely unconventional. He treated us with respect and regarded us as valuable recipients of God's message and salvation. However, what touched me most about that day was his message.

Paul openly shared about the life, message, and mission of Jesus of Nazareth. He said that Jesus went about doing good for all people. He cured those who were sick and others who were possessed by demons. Jesus even raised up the dead. He taught about the imminent arrival of the kingdom of God. His central message was repentance and believing in the Good News. One must forgive and even love one's enemies. However, the religious authorities and the Romans did not find Jesus' message too comforting, so they put him to death by nailing him to a cross. However, God raised him up on the third day. He appeared first to several women, then to the apostles, and then to many other disciples. He even appeared to Paul on the road to Damascus.

....

[20] Jewish sympathizers are attested in some epigraphic and literary sources in antiquity. The primary evidence however comes from Acts of the Apostles: "worshiper of God" (16:14; 18:7); "God-fearing" (10:2, 22; 13:16, 26). Reference about Lydia as a "worshiper of God" in Acts 16:14 indicates that she was a Jewish sympathizer.

Sidebar 7.2
Biblical Backgrounds

What are...*the "we-passages"*?

❖ These are sections found in Acts that are written in the first-person plural. These "we-passages" are found in Acts 16:10–17; 20:5–15; 21:1–18; 27:1—28:16.

❖ The first-person plural narration indicates that the author, Luke, was participating in the events he is describing. He was at times a companion of Paul.

❖ There is no scholarly consensus on the interpretation of these we-passages. Three interpretations are proposed: a) the writer was a genuine historical eyewitness; b) the writer used someone else's travel log and edited them for his traveling narratives; c) the author invented this stylistic device to give more credibility to the narrative.

Paul plainly testified that Jesus of Nazareth is truly the Christ, the one about whom the Scriptures had prophesied and Israel had longed.

Paul went on to say that Jesus Christ is returning very soon to judge the living and the dead. He warned that the end is very near, that "the day of the Lord will come like a thief at night."[21] Paul cautioned about the deception of peace and security that the Roman Empire offered, for disaster will suddenly come upon everyone, "like labor pains upon a pregnant woman, and they will not escape.[22] Unless people repent, change their ways, and believe in God's only Son, they will be condemned to Sheol or a pit of darkness and eternal punishment. But if anyone believes in the Lord Jesus Christ, he or she will become a child of God and hence saved. Paul concluded by reciting this hymn:

....

[21] 1 Thessalonians 5:2. Paul's central message at the early part of his preaching ministry was about the imminent arrival of the day of the Lord. This is attested in his earliest writing found in First Thessalonians.

[22] 1 Thessalonians 5:3. "Peace and security" seemed to have been the common slogan claimed by Rome. Paul obviously defied the complacency of this Roman propaganda.

"Christ Jesus, who, though he was in the form of God, did not regard equality with God something to be grasped. Rather, he emptied himself, taking the form of a slave, coming in human likeness; and found human in appearance, he humbled himself, becoming obedient to death, even death on a cross. Because of this, God greatly exalted him and bestowed on him the name that is above every name, that at the name of Jesus every knee should bend, of those in heaven and on earth and under the earth, and every tongue confess that Jesus Christ is Lord, to the glory of God the Father." [23]

As I listened to the magnificent hymn of Christ, my heart stopped. The Lord Jesus Christ, who was divine and yet gave up his divinity to become a servant, is marvelously powerful beyond all the deities I have ever known. He is transcendent and yet comprehensible. He is both divine and human. Somehow the apparent contradictions did not affect me. Jesus Christ, as testified by Paul, was the Good News I desired to hear and the salvation I longed for. Thus I and my household became believers and were baptized in the water of the Gangites. As a sign of gratitude for the gift of salvation and friendship, I extended an invitation to Paul and his companions to come and stay at my home. At first, they resisted, but I earnestly urged them and eventually prevailed over them.

Gratitude As Christian Virtue

Gratitude is a feeling of thankfulness for blessings or benefits we have received. Gratitude builds humility as we recognize an act of kindness, service, or caring from someone else. True gratitude is a foundation for faith, courage, contentment, happiness, love, and well-being. Gratitude leads us to look outside ourselves and

....

[23] Philippians 2:5–11. This Philippians hymn is believed to be one of the earliest Christological hymns.

turn to the One who bestows such blessings. Numerous studies suggest that grateful people are more likely to have higher levels of happiness and lower levels of stress and depression. It is said that a grateful heart is the beginning of greatness. Experiencing and expressing gratitude is an important aspect of any spiritual practice. Consequently, it is another important trait of a healthy Christian spirituality.

Obviously thankful for her newfound faith, Lydia provided hospitality and a place for Paul and his companions to stay. In the opening verses of his Letter to the Philippians, Paul writes, "I give thanks to my God at every remembrance of you, praying always with joy in my every prayer for all of you, because of your partnership for the gospel from the first day until now. I am confident of this, that the one who began a good work in you will continue to complete it until the day of Christ Jesus" (1:3–6).

At the end of the same letter, Paul extols the Philippian community for their generosity, saying, "You Philippians indeed know that at the beginning of the gospel, when I left Macedonia, not a single church shared with me in an account of giving and receiving, except you alone. For even when I was at Thessalonica you sent me something for my needs, not only once but more than once" (4:15–16). Paul expressed deep gratitude for the Philippians' receptivity and generosity. Although Lydia is not mentioned in the letter, I believe she epitomizes all the qualities mentioned by Paul. Lydia eagerly listened to Paul's words, embraced baptism, and sincerely insisted that Paul and his company stay at her house. She expressed deep gratitude by means of generous hospitality. After Paul was released from prison, Luke records that Paul went to Lydia's house, and it was from there that Paul took leave of the Philippian community (Acts 16:40). Evidently, Lydia, the first recorded European convert, had the qualities necessary to lead the sisters and brothers who gathered under her roof. She had the heart of a true Christian.

A true Christian is one who never forgets to count his or her blessings, particularly what God has done. Gratitude is indeed a Christian virtue. A life of thanksgiving is a life of prayer. The word "Eucharist" comes from the Greek verb *eucharisteo,* which means "to give thanks." Eucharist is essentially an act of thanksgiving for Christ's sacrificial love. Gratitude, the affirmation of a bond between giver and receiver, is central to the human-divine relationship. The author of the Letter to the Colossians encourages his readers by saying, "Let the peace of Christ control your hearts, the peace into which you were also called in one body. And be thankful. Let the word of Christ dwell in you richly, as in all wisdom you teach and admonish one another, singing psalms, hymns, and spiritual songs with gratitude in your hearts to God. And whatever you do, in word or in deed, do everything in the name of the Lord Jesus, giving thanks to God the Father through him" (3:15–17).

The theme of gratitude and thanksgiving is central to Paul's spirituality. Christians ought to give thanks for who God is and what God has done in and through his Son, Jesus Christ. The phrases "be thankful" or "give thanks" occur frequently throughout Paul's letters. Christians are urged to "in all circumstances give thanks" (1 Thessalonians 5:18), give "thanks always and for everything in the name of our Lord Jesus Christ to God the Father" (Ephesians 5:20), and present prayers and petitions "with thanksgiving" to God (Philippians 4:6). To live lives of thanksgiving means acknowledging God's blessings and generosity, which provide a model for how Christians are to relate to one another.

In Judaism, gratitude is an essential part of one's life and devotion to God, for all things come from God. The psalmists constantly emphasize thankfulness and praise. The following list indicates just a few passages from the Book of Psalms that speak about gratitude:

"I will praise you, Lord, with all my heart; I will declare all your wondrous deeds. I will delight and rejoice in you; I will sing hymns to your name, Most High" (9:2–3).

"Give thanks to the Lord, invoke his name; make known among the peoples his deeds! Sing praise to him, play music; proclaim all his wondrous deeds! Glory in his holy name; let hearts that seek the Lord rejoice!" (105:1–3).

"I will praise the Lord with all my heart in the assembled congregation of the upright. Great are the works of the Lord, studied by all who delight in them. Majestic and glorious is his work, his righteousness endures forever" (111:1–3).

"Give thanks to the Lord, for he is good, his mercy endures forever. Let Israel say: his mercy endures forever" (118:1–2).

"Praise the Lord, for he is good; for his mercy endures forever; Praise the God of gods; for his mercy endures forever; Praise the Lord of lords; for his mercy endures forever" (136:1–3).

Expressing gratitude is not a difficult thing. Since it does not cost us anything, we utter the words *thank you* countless times each day. But the question is, "Do we really mean it each time we say it?" That is, in addition to saying "thank you," it is also important to carry out "acts of thanksgiving." In the Gospel of Luke, genuine gratitude often leads to a generous offering of hospitality or sharing of table fellowship. Having been cured of her fever, Simon's mother-in-law "got up immediately and waited on them" (4:39). After responding to Jesus' call to follow him, "Levi gave a great banquet for him in his house" (5:29). Having met Jesus face to face, Zacchaeus, the tax collector, not only invited Jesus into his house and offered him hospitality, but promised to give half of his possessions to the poor and repay four times over anyone from whom he had extorted money (19:8). In the three "lost and found" parables, each one of those who found what was lost responded with a feast or banquet celebrating with neighbors and friends: the Lost Sheep (15:6); the Lost Coin (15:9); and the Lost Son (15:23). On the road to Emmaus, the two disciples invited the stranger for lodging and an evening meal because he had opened up the Scriptures to them and comforted them along the way (24:29). Similarly, Acts of the Apostles records a few examples of genuine expressions of gratitude whereby new converts offered hospitality and/or shared table fellowship: Cornelius (10:49; 11:3), Lydia (16:15), Eutychus (20:11), and Publius (28:10).

Gratitude is an important component in our spirituality and can be a factor in our salvation. In the story of the healing of the Ten Lepers (Luke 17:11–19), Jesus commends the grateful Samaritan while criticizing the indifference of the nine who did not return. As a way to foster healthy spirituality, we must train ourselves to express thankfulness both in words and in actions. Finally, we should remember the words of Jesus, who says, "It is more blessed to give than to receive" (Acts 20:35).

Points for Reflection

- Luke says, "The Lord opened her [Lydia's] heart to pay attention to what Paul was saying" (Acts 16:14). What in your heart needs to be opened to hear what God is saying to you today?

- Experiencing and expressing gratitude is an important trait of a healthy spirituality. What are three things for which you are most thankful? How can you show that you have been blessed?

- The words of Jesus are seldom recorded outside the Gospels, yet Acts retains Jesus' precious saying, "It is more blessed to give than to receive." Can you give an example to demonstrate the truth of Jesus' profound statement?

Paul in Athens

The second half of the Acts of the Apostles focuses on the missionary work of the Apostle Paul. Luke records three important missionary journeys whereby Paul and his companions traveled to many distant shores, traversed over a huge landmass that covered thousands of miles, and founded many Christian communities.[24] Paul's missionary activities fulfill Jesus' commission, "You will be my witnesses in Jerusalem, throughout Judea and Samaria, and to the ends of the earth" (Acts 1:8b). Many readily embrace the Good News, but some resist and strongly oppose. There are stories of success as well as failure. One story stands out. The story of a gentile convert from Athens will intersect with our life and can teach us a lot about the tolerance of diversity.

What do we do when the people we minister to are disinterested or even hostile? How do we go about telling the story of Jesus in a way that might engage the listener on his or her own ground? The story of Paul in Athens, especially his sermon at the Areopagus, can teach us much about preaching to a hostile audience and about inculturation. We will hear from an eyewitness, who was actually converted through Paul's preaching in Athens. His name is Dionysius the Areopagite. But let us pause for a moment to read Acts 17:16–34. As you read, ponder this

....

[24] Paul's first journey took place in 44–48 (Acts 13:1—14:28); the second journey in 49–52 (Acts 15:36—18:22); and the third took place in 53–57 (Acts 18:23—20:38).

question: How does Paul's sermon to the Athenians intersect with some of today's philosophies that deal with God, life, death, the afterlife, and evil?

> While Paul was waiting for them in Athens, he grew exasperated at the sight of the city full of idols. So he debated in the synagogue with the Jews and with the worshipers, and daily in the public square with whoever happened to be there. Even some of the Epicurean and Stoic philosophers engaged him in discussion. Some asked, "What is this scavenger trying to say?" Others said, "He sounds like a promoter of foreign deities," because he was preaching about "Jesus" and "Resurrection." They took him and led him to the Areopagus and said, "May we learn what this new teaching is that you speak of? For you bring some strange notions to our ears; we should like to know what these things mean." Now all the Athenians as well as the foreigners residing there used their time for nothing else but telling or hearing something new.

> Then Paul stood up at the Areopagus and said: "You Athenians, I see that in every respect you are very religious. For as I walked around looking carefully at your shrines, I even discovered an altar inscribed, 'To an Unknown God.' What therefore you unknowingly worship, I proclaim to you. The God who made the world and all that is in it, the Lord of heaven and earth, does not dwell in sanctuaries made by human hands, nor is he served by human hands because he needs anything. Rather it is he who gives to everyone life and breath and everything. He made from one the whole human race to dwell on the entire surface of the earth, and he fixed the ordered seasons and the boundaries of their regions, so that people might seek God, even perhaps grope for him and find him, though indeed he is not far from any one of us. For 'In him we live and move and have our being,' as even some of your poets have said, 'For we too are his

offspring.' Since therefore we are the offspring of God, we ought not to think that the divinity is like an image fashioned from gold, silver, or stone by human art and imagination. God has overlooked the times of ignorance, but now he demands that all people everywhere repent because he has established a day on which he will 'judge the world with justice' through a man he has appointed, and he has provided confirmation for all by raising him from the dead." When they heard about resurrection of the dead, some began to scoff, but others said, "We should like to hear you on this some other time." And so Paul left them. But some did join him, and became believers. Among them were Dionysius, a member of the Court of the Areopagus, a woman named Damaris, and others with them.

Dionysius, the Open-minded Areopagite

My name is Dionysius the Areopagite. I was a member and judge of the Areopagus. I was converted to Christianity by the preaching of the Apostle Paul during his Areopagus sermon. The Areopagus, or in Greek *Areios Pagos* ("Rock of Ares"), is located on the northwestern side of the Acropolis, which in ancient Athens functioned as the high court of appeal for criminal and civil cases. During Paul's time, this rocky hill was referred to by the Romans as "Mars Hill," which was a platform for discussing matters pertaining to religious life of the city. Curious about the disturbing new message being echoed around the city, the Council of Areopagus summoned Paul to present his case and to hear about a new movement called "The Way." Since I happened to be a member of that high council, I was there when Paul delivered his sermon. But first, allow me to tell you a little about my beloved city and its inhabitants.

Athens, which was the heart of Greek culture and philosophy, is the city that produced great philosophers like Socrates, Pericles,

Sidebar 8.1
Biblical Characters

Who is...*Dionysius the Areopagite*?

❖ He was a judge or member of the Court of the Areopagus. He was converted through the preaching of the Apostle Paul during his Areopagus sermon (Acts 17:22–34).

❖ According to tradition, he became a bishop of Athens and was martyred for his faith.

❖ His feast day is October 9. He is considered the patron of lawyers.

and Plato. It is widely referred to as the cradle of Western civilization and the birthplace of democracy. Although Athens was well past its golden age by the time Paul arrived, it was still considered the greatest university city of its time, and intellectuals from all over the Roman Empire were drawn to it. One customary activity of the Athenian intellectuals was to gather in public squares and marketplaces to argue and debate any new thing or idea that surfaced. Different groups argued and defended their philosophies. Some espoused a philosophy called Epicureanism, which teaches that gods were remote from the world and didn't particularly care about what was going on in it. The evidence of suffering in the world strengthened their argument. The Stoics, however, argued that everything came from the mind of Zeus and therefore human beings have no control over life or death but simply live at the whim of the gods. For the Stoics, everything is predetermined; human beings have no freedom whatsoever.

But Athens was more than an intellectual city; it was also a religious center for worship. Temples and shrines dedicated to all sorts of gods and goddesses existed throughout the city. The Greeks had a god for every occasion. There was Ares, the god of war; and Aphrodite, the goddess of love. There was Hestia, the goddess of fire; and Poseidon, the god of the sea. There was Athena, the goddess of wisdom; and Nike, the god of victory. There was Dionysus, the god of wine; and Asclepius, the god of healing. At every turn and in practically every niche one could find statues of idols, gods, and goddesses made of marble, gold, bronze, or wood in all shapes and sizes. There was even a shrine dedicated to an unknown god.

Paul arrived in Athens on a cool, sunny spring day in the year 51. The Acropolis and the *agora* (marketplace) were bustling with people and general commotion. Paul had just come from the north, leaving Luke, Timothy, and Silas behind to care for the newly founded communities. Paul had caused an uproar in many of the towns and cities he had previously visited, such as Philippi, Thessalonica, and Beroea. In Thessalonica his friends had to slip him away in the night to safety. His opponents pursued him wherever he went. Paul hoped that in a bigger city like Athens, he might be able to elude his opponents a little more easily.

When Paul arrived in Athens, he was alone and a stranger in a big city. As was his custom, or *modus operandi* in Latin, he sought out the *agora*, the busiest part of the city, to rent a shop. These storefront shops, called *insulae*[25], were very popular in our time. One could find almost anything to purchase there. I love to wander these shops, looking for new gadgets, precious artifacts, and antiques. The ancient *agora* is similar to your modern shopping malls or outlet stores. The difference is that these *insulae* usually have sleeping quarters above them; furthermore, along the shops, the *cardos* (or streets) are beautifully decorated with columns, marble pavements, and mosaics. Since Paul was a tentmaker and a leather craftsman, he was very good with his hands. He could do magic with a piece of leather, using only a needle and thread. Since tents were constantly in demand for local dwellers and travelers, and since leather goods such as sandals, bags, purses,

....

[25] These ancient complexes, which are similar to modern tenement buildings or commercial complexes, are still visible today at the archaeological ruins in Ostia (Italy) and Corinth (Greece).

belts, and hats are basic necessities for daily living, Paul's shop was well visited by many passersby. He seemed to work day and night. I stumbled into his shop purely by accident. One day while going down from the Acropolis, the straps on my sandals broke, so I came to his shop to get them repaired. Since that day, I have returned almost daily to listen to him talk about the man called Jesus the Christ, who died but rose from the dead. What I heard and discovered in that shop changed my life forever.

Ever since the age of reason, I had pondered and followed various philosophies and worshiped many gods and goddesses. There was a period when I followed the teaching of Epicureanism, which claims there is no god. When being an atheist didn't satisfy my intellectual curiosity and reasoning, I picked up Stoicism. The belief in predetermination and that human beings have no freedom didn't seem right to me either. Since philosophy didn't satisfy all my longings, I turned to religion by worshiping different gods and goddesses. My favorite was Dionysus, the god of wine and gladness, and the name given to me by my parents, Dionysius. However, being a judge of the Council of Areopagus, I needed a lot of wisdom and guidance from the gods, so I frequently prayed to the goddess Athena. I even have a shrine to her set up in my house.

Since every aspect of our life was under the purview of some god or goddess, it was natural for us to seek out the gods for assistance and protection. Revering the right god or goddess for the right occasion is the key to fortune and blessings. But after meeting Paul and hearing the story of the life and message of Jesus Christ from Nazareth, everything began to make sense to me. The God of Jesus Christ isn't remote from human affairs. God actually reached out to the world and made the first move. God so loved the world that God sent his beloved Son to save the world from corruption and sin. However, his people did not accept him and put him to death by means of crucifixion, but God raised him up on the third day. Paul talked much about Jesus Christ as the *Logos*, or Wisdom, who existed from the beginning, was with God, and is God. What the tentmaker from Tarsus said made sense to me. There must be only one God in whom we believe, move, and have our being; otherwise, life is meaningless and empty.

While all the conversations I had with Paul in his shop made a lot of sense to me, I was not completely convinced until that marvelous sermon on the Areopagus. That speech helped pull everything together. It answered all my philosophical questions and dispelled every doubt I ever had about the existence of God. Paul seemed to have done his homework well. He had studied and understood our philosophies; he knew about all our gods. He was also familiar with our culture and customs. He understood our way of thinking and being. To use your modern terminology, he had "inculturated" well.

> **Sidebar 8.2**
> **Biblical Backgrounds**
>
> **What is...*epicureanism?***
>
> ❖ It is a system of philosophy based on the teachings of Epicurus, founded around 307 BCE.
>
> ❖ It emphasizes the neutrality of the gods that they do not interfere with human lives. It teaches that gods, matter, and souls are all made of atoms. It rejects immortality and any possibility of an afterlife.
>
> ❖ It propounded a philosophy and an ethic of individual pleasure as the sole or chief good in life.
>
> ❖ Epicureanism flourished in the late Hellenistic era and during the Roman era. By the end of the Roman era and having undergone Christian attack and repression, it eventually died out.

The words he spoke were very familiar to us Athenians. He quoted Greek poets and philosophers. The words he used, "The God who made the world and all that is in it" (Acts 17:24), come straight out of Stoic philosophy. The phrase, "In him we live and move and have our being" (v. 28) is a quotation from a Greek philosopher named Epimenides. The line, "For we too are his offspring" (v. 28), comes from Aratus, a well-known Greek poet. To involve us even more in his argument and discourse, he complimented the religious atmosphere of our cultural milieu, saying, "I see that in every respect you are very religious" (v. 22). He mentioned an altar with the inscription, "To an Unknown God" (v. 23). Paul engaged us Athenians by using our own philosophies and practices to make a point. He spoke a language we could understand.

I was not only captivated but completely convinced with his Good News and became a believer that day. A woman named Damaris and a few others were also converted. Many others, however, were not convinced. Some sneered, while others walked away in disbelief over the issue of the resurrection of the dead. As for me, I am forever changed, thanks to the great Apostle Paul for having introduced me to the Good News of the Lord Jesus Christ!

Tolerance of Diversity As Healthy Attitude

What impressed me about Paul's speech at the Areopagus was his tolerance and respectful attitude toward the Athenians. Even though Paul was greatly distressed by the many idols, he did not chastise them for their beliefs. He did not mock their idols nor was he judgmental and self-righteous. Paul had taken the time to look around and get the "feel" of their culture and beliefs, including the altar of the Unknown God. Though Paul did not spend a lot of time criticizing their idols, he did point out that they were images made by human design and skill. Notice also how Paul gently corrected them, saying "we" instead of the more accusatory "you" (verses 28–29). The thrust of Paul's speech was to call them to turn from evil ways and invite them to worship the true God. For Paul, Jesus fulfills all righteousness and therefore was raised from the dead. At the mention of the resurrection of Christ, some sneered, and some believed. As a culture, Greeks in general were not interested in the resurrection of the body.

They would have considered it an absurd notion. Nevertheless, Paul's speech was not completely unsuccessful. First, the Athenians did not violently oppose Paul's argument and belief. They considered hearing him "some other time" (v. 32). Second, a few people believed: Dionysius, a member of the Court of Areopagus; a woman named Damaris; and others with them.

There is great diversity among human beings. We are a "mixed bag," or motley race, and no two people are the same. We are physically different in skin color, size, and body structure. We differ also in the ways we think, feel, and believe. Our customs and cultural practices are quite diverse and unique. I belong to an international religious missionary congregation, ministering in over seventy countries on the planet. Residing with people from many parts of the globe, I can attest that multicultural living is not easy. One of the greatest challenges of community life is learning to appreciate the differences we find in one another and not see them as threats. To cherish the diversity of God's array of manifold gifts, one must have a healthy dose of tolerance. Moreover, as Melannie Svoboda states, "A healthy spirituality should lead us to celebrate our differences and to see them as a reflection of God's beneficence and creativity." [26]

Tolerance is accepting customs or attitudes that are different from our own. Consequently, to be tolerant, we do not have to give up who we are. We do not have to compromise our personal beliefs. We do not even have to agree with everything another says. It is purely the act of accepting that others have the right to feel the way they do, just as we have that same right.

While diversity is a gift and a blessing, it is also a challenge. A 1999 report from the United Nations shows a significant rise in religious extremism and intolerance throughout the world. The report provides examples of overt and covert discrimination

....

[26] Melannie Svoboda, SND, *Traits of a Healthy Spirituality* (Mystic, CT: Twenty-Third Publications, 1997), 41.

against Christianity, Islam, and many other religious groups.[27] How tolerant are you of diversity? Do you see diversity as blessing or curse, gift or nuisance, grace or threat?

Scripture speaks much about diversity and clearly presents it as a good thing. In the Creation stories found in the Book of Genesis, God creates a wide variety of things: light and darkness, sun and moon, oceans and dry land, birds and fish, trees and plants. God fashioned man and woman in God's own image. And God pronounced this array of assorted things and beings "very good!" The words of the psalmist reiterate very well, "I praise you, because I am wonderfully made; wonderful are your works! My very self you know" (139:14).

The prophet Micah prophesied about a coming time when nations would stop making weapons of war. Furthermore, the various peoples of the world will live in peace and pursue their different religions, each worshiping their different gods and goddesses. Here is what Micah says, "They shall beat their swords into plowshares, and their spears into pruning hooks; one nation shall not raise the sword against another, nor shall they train for war again. They shall all sit under their own vines, under their own fig trees, undisturbed; for the LORD of hosts has spoken. Though all the peoples walk, each in the name of its god, we will walk in the name of the LORD, our God, forever and ever" (4:3–5).

Jesus, too, promoted religious tolerance in his teaching and ministry. While the disciples forbade the man to heal in Jesus' name, Jesus did not approve the disciples' action. The Gospel of Mark records the incident in this way: "John said to [Jesus], 'Teacher, we saw someone driving out demons in your name, and we tried to prevent him because he does not follow us.' Jesus replied, 'Do not prevent him. There is no one who performs a

....

[27] See ipsnews.net/1999/12/religion-rights-religious-extremism-on-the-rise-says-un/ (accessed on June 3, 2013).

mighty deed in my name who can at the same time speak ill of me. For whoever is not against us is for us'" (9:38–40). When the inhabitants of a village in Samaria rejected his teachings, Jesus not only refused to grant the disciples' request to curse the nonbelievers but reprimanded them for their evil intention. The incident is recorded in the Gospel of Luke: "When the disciples James and John saw this they asked, 'Lord, do you want us to call down fire from heaven to consume them?' Jesus turned and rebuked them, and they journeyed to another village" (9:54–56). Noticeably, Jesus responded to the situation by simply moving on to the next village.

Jesus not only taught about tolerance of diversity in people, but he lived and practiced it. Jesus chose twelve apostles, who came from different walks of life. Several were fishermen from small villages, one was a tax collector, another was a religious zealot. They were quite a heterogeneous group (Mark 3:13–19). Some were married, and others may have been single. Jesus' disciples also included women. Some of these women had elite status, with resources to support his ministry (Luke 8:1–3). Jesus reached out to all types of people: friends and foes, rich and poor, Jews and Greeks, saints and sinners. Jesus looked beyond the differences of gender, age, personality, ethnicity, and religious beliefs. He respected the uniqueness of each individual and accepted each person as she/he is. Noticeably, Jesus' parables of the kingdom can be appreciated by listeners of diverse background and profession. To farmers he spoke in images of fields and wheat, to housewives in images of bread-making and housecleaning, to builders in images of stone and mortar, to fishermen in images of net and fishes, to merchants in images of pearls and treasures.

However, it is Jesus' teaching on love that challenges and stretches our understanding of diversity most profoundly and directly.[28] The followers of Christ must not only love their neighbors as themselves; they are to love even their enemies:

> You have heard that it was said, "You shall love your neighbor and hate your enemy." But I say to you, love your enemies, and pray for those who persecute you, that you may be children of your heavenly Father, for he makes his sun rise on the bad and the good, and causes rain to fall on the just and the unjust. For if you love those who love you, what recompense will you have? Do not the tax collectors do the same? And if you greet your brothers only, what is unusual about that? Do not the pagans do the same? So be perfect, just as your heavenly Father is perfect (Matthew 5:43–48).

Jesus' commandment to love our enemies is a concrete example to demonstrate our tolerance for diversity. Allow me to end this section with a prayer based on 1 Corinthians 13:3–8:

> Lord,
> teach us the true meaning of love
> and also give us grace to practice it,
> for if we have no love we are nothing:
>
> Love is patient and kind and envies no one.
>
> Love is never boastful or conceited or rude.
>
> Love is never selfish or quick to take offense.
>
> Love does not rejoice in wrong but rejoices in right.
>
> Love is always eager to believe the best,
> always hopeful, always patient.
>
> Love is eternal, for love is God and God is love.[29]

....

[28] Svoboda, *Traits*, 41.

[29] Frank Colquhoun, *Prayers for Today* (Philadelphia, PA: Triangle Publications, 1989), 46.

Points for Reflection

- Paul engaged the people of Athens by using their own language and philosophies to establish a common ground with them. He entered into their culture and spoke words they could understand. How might you connect with others to engage them in your faith and understanding of the Good News of Jesus Christ?

- The story of Paul in Athens challenges us to open our eyes to the unexpected ways in which we might experience God's presence in our lives. What are some memorable surprises you have encountered in your life? Will you let yourself be surprised today?

- Paul's Areopagus sermon teaches us much about tolerance of diversity. Do you consider tolerance a characteristic of a healthy spirituality? How can you be more tolerant with others?

Priscilla and Aquila

A cts of the Apostles recounts the deeds of Peter, Paul, and many other disciples, such as Stephen, Philip, John, Barnabas, Timothy, and Silas. Since all of them are male disciples, some people mistakenly think women have little or no role in the building and expansion of the Church. Furthermore, since all of them are single men, married couples seem to have no involvement in the mission of the Church until we meet Priscilla and Aquila. This immigrant missionary couple was constantly on the move for the cause of the gospel and ministered in three important early Christian communities. They first settled in Rome, were then forced to migrate to Corinth because of the Edict of Claudius in 49, relocated in Ephesus for the purpose of evangelization, and finally returned to Rome after Claudius's death in 54. They relocated both their home and their trade at least three times in three different sites. Their home was as movable as the tents they produced. Yet, they never faltered in their commitment to preach the Gospel of Jesus Christ, risking everything because of their faith.

Priscilla and Aquila were models of conjugal and lay missionary life. They were greatly appreciated by "all the churches of the gentiles," said Paul (Romans 16:4). Consequently, it is no surprise that this extraordinary couple was remembered and honored by two different New Testament authors: Luke (Acts 18:2–3, 18, 26) and Paul (1 Corinthians 16:19; Romans 16:3; 2 Timothy 4:19). In order to understand and appreciate the impact made by this immigrant missionary couple, we can let Priscilla, who was seemingly more influential than her husband, recount their faith journey. Her story will help us see the importance of friendship in ministry, which is another important trait of a healthy spirituality. But first, pause to read the following passages concerning Priscilla and Aquila found in the Acts of the Apostles:

> After this [Paul] left Athens and went to Corinth. There he met a Jew named Aquila, a native of Pontus, who had recently come from Italy with his wife Priscilla because Claudius had ordered all the Jews to leave Rome. He went to visit them and, because he practiced the same trade, stayed with them and worked, for they were tentmakers by trade. (18:1–3)

> Paul remained for quite some time, and after saying farewell to the brothers he sailed for Syria, together with Priscilla and Aquila. At Cenchreae he had his hair cut because he had taken a vow. When they reached Ephesus, he left them there, while he entered the synagogue and held discussions with the Jews. (18:18–19)

> A Jew named Apollos, a native of Alexandria, an eloquent speaker, arrived in Ephesus. He was an authority on the scriptures. He had been instructed in the Way of the Lord and, with ardent spirit, spoke and taught accurately about Jesus, although he knew only the baptism of John. He began to speak boldly in the synagogue; but when Priscilla and Aquila heard him, they took him aside and explained to him the Way (of God) more accurately. And when he wanted to cross to Achaia, the brothers encouraged him and wrote to the disciples there to welcome him. After his arrival he gave great assistance to those who had come to believe through grace. (18:24–27)

Priscilla, the Migrant Missionary "Apostle"

It was a pleasant spring day in the year 50 when my husband and I first arrived in Corinth. I was exhausted from the arduous journey. We had walked through miles of rugged terrain on the *Via Appia* and then sailed over the raging waters of the Mediterranean Sea during the winter season when ships weren't supposed to sail. We had spent too many sleepless and chilly nights under the open sky. The distance from Rome to Corinth was over 600 miles, so making the journey was not a small feat for a city woman like me. I was physically exhausted and emotionally traumatized. I was expelled from my house and the city I had grown to love. I became a refugee, living far away from my family and friends. I lost much, all because of my faith. Due to a disturbance incited by some Jews and Christians over the issue of Jesus being the Christ, the emperor Claudius had intervened to maintain "law and order" and decreed an edict ordering those who were involved to leave Rome.[30] As a result, many Jews as well as Christians were expelled from the Eternal City. My husband and I were among the exiles. The incident took place in the year 49.

Since my husband was from Pontus, we decided to return to his birthplace, and so we headed in that direction. However, when we arrived in Corinth, we changed our plans and decided to stay

....

[30] Several important questions loom concerning the Edict of Claudius, namely, what was the cause of the expulsion, who was expelled, and how many? These questions cannot be resolved easily, and consensus among scholars cannot be reached. Reliable historical sources indicate that approximately twenty to thirty thousand Jews might have been in Rome at the time Claudius expelled Priscilla and Aquila. To expel "all Jews," as Luke records it, would have caused disorder and a logistical nightmare. Thus, I agree with some historians that only (and perhaps only certain) Christian Jews, or possibly only "ringleaders," were expelled from Rome, but probably not all.

a while because the Isthmian Games were being celebrated that year in Isthmia, which is only walking distance from Corinth.[31] We rented an *insula* and set up a leather business, fixing tents and other leather goods, which were in great demand by travelers all over the empire gathering for the Isthmian Games. Although business was good, the work was very demanding, for I was not yet accustomed to the heavy needle and palm work of tentmakers. I could hardly wait until the games were over so we could move on. Corinth, a great commercial city with a double harbor, was not the sort of place for Christians to be. Corinth was notorious for its licentiousness and loose morality. But God had a different plan for us. We met a man named Paul from Tarsus.

Paul had just left Athens, where he had met some stiff opposition and was hauled before the Court of the Areopagus to explain his teachings. He came to Corinth not really expecting to find any followers of Christ in this disreputable and immoral city, but God led him into our shop that day looking for work, because he too was a tentmaker. After discovering who we were and why we left Rome,[32] Paul was greatly encouraged and began to tell his story. He had been an ardent persecutor of the Way, but having met the risen Lord on the road to Damascus, he was converted. Since then, he had traveled to many cities and towns, proclaiming the Good News of Christ and founding many communities. He also told us about the vision of the Macedonian

....

[31] Isthmian Games were held every two years in Isthmia. They did not coincide with the cycle of the Olympic Games, which recurred every four years.

[32] I believe Priscilla and Aquila were already Christians before they arrived at Corinth. Moreover, the likely reason for their expulsion was because they were leaders of the Christian community in Rome. Paul's farewell address in Romans 16:5 indicates that the Christian community in Rome was gathering in their home.

man pleading with him to come over to Europe, and that was how he ended up in Corinth. We offered him work and shelter, and from that day on, we became partners in Christ. We worked night and day convincing those who came to our shop that Jesus was the Christ.

Together with Paul, we established an *ecclesia*, or assembly. There were only a handful of us in the beginning. Nevertheless, we gathered regularly in the upper room of our shop to break bread and to teach about the Way and the Good News of Jesus Christ. To our amazement, the community grew quickly. Even Crispus, the synagogue official, came to believe in the Lord, along with his entire household. Eventually, our upstairs apartment could no longer accommodate the whole church. The community had to be divided. Some remained with us in our house church, while others went with Paul to the house of Titus Justus, whose house was next to a synagogue.

**Sidebar 9.1
Biblical Characters**

Who are...*Priscilla and Aquila*?

❖ Priscilla (also known as Prisca) and her husband Aquila were tentmakers, "co-workers" of Paul and Timothy, and founders (or co-founders) of the churches in Corinth and Ephesus.

❖ They were expelled from Rome in the year 49 because of the Edict of Claudius.

❖ They were mentors and catechizers of the great preacher Apollos and many others, and hosts of the local church in their own home in Corinth, Ephesus, and Rome.

❖ Priscilla and Aquila are regarded as saints by several Christian Churches. They are celebrated in the Roman Church on July 8, in the Greek Orthodox Church on February 13, and in the Lutheran Church with their pupil Apollos on February 13.

❖ Biblical references pertaining to them are found in Luke (Acts 18:1–3, 18–19, 26–27), Paul (1 Cor 16:19; Rom 16:3) and Timothy (2 Tm 4:19).

We had one incident that happened when Gallio was proconsul of Achaia. Sosthenes, the synagogue official, and other Jews rose up and accused Paul of false teachings. They brought him before the tribunal. Since the issue dealt with religious matters and not some crime or malicious fraud, the proconsul refused to intervene and literally drove them away from the tribunal. Apart from this incident of accusation before Gallio, the community prospered and was at peace.

After working with Paul for eighteen months to build up the church in Corinth, it was time for us to pack up and move on. With basic portable tools (awl, needles, and thread), we were able to relocate with ease. The Corinthian church was still in its infant stage, but it was well on its way. We could only hope and trust in the work of the Holy Spirit. Paul, too, had decided it was time to return to Syria. After saying our farewell to the brothers and sisters, many of whom we had come to cherish and love, we went to the port at Cenchreae. From there, we sailed across the Aegean Sea and landed in Ephesus, the leading capital of Asia Minor. After a brief rest in Ephesus, Paul continued on to Jerusalem to visit with the members of the church there, and then returned to Antioch. As for my husband and me, we settled in Ephesus.

Ephesus was steeped in philosophy and religion. It was the center of learning, with a library containing countless precious scrolls. It was also the center for worship of Artemis, the mother goddess who is the patron of pregnant women. Her home, the temple of Artemis, was located in Ephesus and was considered one of the Seven Wonders of the World. Ephesus was also a city for commerce. The city's seaport provided a means for goods to come in and go out. The city attracted intellectuals, merchants, and pilgrims from all over the Roman Empire. There was plenty of opportunity here. As had become our custom, we rented an *insula* and set up our leather business. While Aquila focused more on the financial and business side of things, I concentrated more on the proclamation of the Gospel. It was our unspoken agreement. I took every opportunity I had to spread the Good News of Christ, whether in the synagogue debating with my Jewish people or with newcomers who visited our shop. Similar to what had happened in Corinth, our home eventually became a "house church" for catechism and for fellowship meals.

One day a man from the Jewish community in Alexandria came to Ephesus. He was a scholar and an eloquent and persuasive speaker. He spoke in the synagogue, and when I heard him, I realized that, learned as he was, he did not know the full story of Jesus. Thus, I took him

> **Sidebar 9.2**
> **Biblical Backgrounds**
>
> **What is...the Edict of Claudius?**
>
> ❖ A decree made by the Roman emperor named Claudius in the year 49 expelling many people (Jews and Christian Jews) from Rome because of some disturbances concerning Christ or *impulsore Chresto* (at the instigation of Chrestus).
>
> ❖ The biblical reference to this event is found in Acts 18:1–2.
>
> ❖ Priscilla and Aquila were among those Christian Jews who were expelled from Rome.

aside and taught him more accurately about what Jesus did, said, and taught. Apollos stayed with us for some time. After having been well informed about the Way, he moved on to Achaia and eventually ended up in Corinth.[33]

After some time, Paul rejoined us in Ephesus during his third missionary journey. When he arrived, the stage had already been set. Together with Paul, we were able to accomplish many good things, and the community grew a little stronger and more numerous each day. Paul was passionate. His zeal and commitment to the proclamation of the Gospel were infectious. We worked night and day teaching and encouraging the new converts in the faith. We were also concerned with some of the issues and crises that were coming up in other communities. News about the brothers and sisters in Corinth concerning their immoral-

....

[33] Acts 19:1. See also 1 Corinthians 1:10–12.

ity and division occupied Paul's thoughts. Since he could not go there to resolve the crises, he would write to them. It was a very useful way to respond to the immediate issues, but it could easily cause misunderstanding since a letter cannot replace a personal visit to explain things more fully.

In the fall of the year 54, we received news that the emperor Claudius had died. With his death, the Edict of Claudius was lifted, and therefore we could finally return to our home in Rome. The news brought me much comfort. Aquila and I had been living on the road for more than four years. Our migration led us to many places and gave us many opportunities to witness to our faith in the Lord. We met many faith-filled people and had the privilege to collaborate with the great Apostle Paul, but it was time to return home. As I embarked from the port of Ephesus, I wondered what else God had in store for my husband and me.

Friendship As Gospel Value

Our spiritual journey requires close friends for support and guidance, whether they are our spouse, a spiritual companion, a co-worker, or a mentor. The Book of Proverbs writes, "A brother offended is more unyielding than a stronghold; such strife is more daunting than castle gates" (18:19). The Bible includes many examples of friendship: Abraham and God (Isaiah 41:8; James 2:23); David and Jonathan (1 Samuel 18:1–3); Elijah and Elisha (2 Kings 2:2); Ruth and Naomi (Ruth 1:16–17). Paul had many close friends who accompanied him on his missionary journeys and collaborated with him in mission, including Barnabas, Luke, John Mark, Titus, Timothy, Silas, Lydia, Apollos, Phoebe, and Priscilla and Aquila. When we turn to Romans 16, we are pleasantly surprised at the long list of men and women with whom Paul collaborated in his ministry, and that's from only one letter. Many other friends and co-workers appear in other epistles. Throughout his mission endeavor, Paul obviously relied on close friends as co-workers. Priscilla and Aquila were some of Paul's most faithful friends.

Acts tells us that Paul met up with this migrant couple from Rome in Corinth and resided in their home. The three worked together as tentmakers and as collaborators in building up the church in Corinth (18:1–3). Having spent eighteen months working side by side in Corinth (18:11), they accompanied Paul on a 250-mile journey across the Aegean Sea to Ephesus. Luke says that Paul left them at Ephesus as soon as they arrived, which indicates the migrant couple must have founded the church in Ephesus and prepared the stage for Paul when he rejoined them on his third missionary journey.

Paul himself made two significant references to his friends. The first occurrence is found in the farewell greetings of the letter to the Corinthian church. The detail mentioned by Paul in his address, "together with the church at their house" (1 Corinthians 16:19) could very well indicate that Paul resided in their home at Ephesus when he wrote 1 Corinthians. Paul's second reference about his friends occurs in the farewell greetings of the Letter to the Romans (16:3–5). The letter was probably written in 56 or 57, when Priscilla and Aquila had already returned to Rome.[34] In this brief description, Paul highlights four outstanding features about this missionary couple. First, Paul regards them as his "co-workers in Christ Jesus." Second, they risked "their necks" for his life, perhaps because they had defended Paul and remained faithful to him. Third, Paul and "all the churches of the gentiles" are grateful to them. And fourth, believers are meeting in their home in Rome,[35] just as they had while they were in Ephesus and

....

[34] The couple, along with other Judean Christ believers, could have returned soon after the death of Claudius in the fall of 54.

[35] The church of Prisc(ill)a and Aquila in Rome is built on top of an ancient house church believed to have been the home of this missionary couple. Inside the church is a fresco depicting Peter baptizing Priscilla.

in Corinth.[36] Clearly, Paul did not work alone in the mission field but often relied on and collaborated with Priscilla and Aquila in ministry. In his close ties with this migrant missionary couple, Paul teaches that human friendship should always be cherished and viewed as a gospel value.

When we examine the Synoptic Gospels, we are also pleasantly surprised to see that Jesus had many friends and was not afraid to show affection toward them. From the Twelve Apostles whom he had chosen, he had three close confidants: Peter, James, and John. Jesus was also accompanied by women who provided for him and his disciples from their own resources. Jesus found shelter and hospitality in the house of the sisters Mary and Martha. Jesus frequently ate with friends and enjoyed spending time in their company.

Challenges and difficulties in ministry are not uncommon. If we do our work correctly or genuinely, we are likely to encounter resistance and opposition. Jesus even admits that "no prophet is welcomed in his or her native place." Because of this reality, we need support and lots of encouragement from close friends. Jesus knew how important friendship was in his ministerial life. Perhaps that is why Jesus sent the disciples out on their missionary journey in pairs so that together they would support each other, especially in those inhospitable and hostile situations.

....

[36] 2 Timothy (4:19) also has a reference concerning Priscilla and Aquila. The author of this letter sends greetings to Priscilla and Aquila who are depicted as "faithfully ministering with Timothy in Ephesus." The letter to 1 Timothy (1:3) indicates that Timothy resides in Ephesus. From this seemingly insignificant reference, we are informed that by late first century or early second century, when these pastoral letters were written, the missionary couple had once again immigrated to Ephesus. Furthermore, being listed first in the greetings testifies to the enormous respect and regard the author and early believers had for them.

The theme of friendship is repeatedly highlighted in the Gospel of John. Jesus loved Lazarus and Mary and Martha. At the death of Lazarus, Jesus wept. Even in a state of mourning, Martha ran out to meet Jesus at the edge of town and professed that he is the resurrection and life. Her sister Mary also sought Jesus out in time of mourning and found much solace in his presence. Before Jesus' passion and death, Mary anointed her teacher and friend with expensive perfume to prepare for his burial. Indeed, Jesus frequently stayed with this family in Bethany, enjoying precious moments of hospitality and experiencing deep friendship.

The theme of friendship is also evident in the farewell discourse of the Gospel of John. In those last hours on earth, Jesus called his disciples friends: "I no longer call you slaves, because a slave does not know what his master is doing. I have called you friends, because I have told you everything I have heard from my Father" (15:15). Jesus treated the disciples as true friends and never as servants. Having been sent by the Father, he entrusted to them everything he had heard and experienced from his Abba, or Father. Jesus says, "For God so loved the world that he gave his only Son, so that everyone who believes in him might not perish but might have eternal life" (3:16). Just as the Father has loved the Son, so Jesus also loved his disciples. Furthermore, Jesus demonstrated the ultimate proof of his capacity for friendship in his readiness to die for his friends: "No one has greater love than this, to lay down one's life for one's friends" (15:13).

Before he entered into his passion and death, Jesus showed deep affection and found much solace in reclining next to or (more accurately from the Greek) in the bosom of his closest friend, the "one whom Jesus loved" (John 13:23). The Gospel of John speaks much about the disciple whom Jesus loved. This disciple remained at the foot of the cross to be with Jesus at the most painful moments of his earthly life. His presence also gave comfort to Mary, his Mother, and the other women. Even though most of his friends deserted him, Jesus did not give up on their friendship. Instead, after his resurrection, he gave friendship another chance by forgiving those friends who had abandoned him. Peter, who had denied him three times, was allowed to redeem himself by publicly attesting three times, "You know that I love you!" (John 21:17).

To seek to be like Jesus includes imitating his ability to befriend people. Furthermore, the ability to share deep friendship with others is a distinguishing mark of being a believer. The author of Sirach writes, "Faithful friends are a sturdy shelter; whoever finds one finds a treasure. Faithful friends are beyond price, no amount can balance their worth" (6:14–15). I'll end this section with this prayer:

Dear God,
thank you for being my faithful friend
and for giving me good friends
with whom I can share insight, interest, or affection.

Thank you for sending friends and companions on the journey
to help me discover who I am and expand my outlook in life.

They have embodied your unconditional love
to guide, challenge, and encourage me along the path of life.

God, help me to treasure my friends as you have loved me,
with kindness, patience, trust, and sensitivity.

May I learn to make sacrifices for my friends
and even to lay down my life for them
just as you have done for me.

I ask this through the intercession of all those who
befriended you while you walked on this marvelous planet.

Amen.

Points for Reflection

- Priscilla and her husband, Aquila, were close friends and supporters of Paul, and as such were founding members of the Christian Church. Priscilla and Aquila were great team players. Ask yourself these questions: Do I prefer to work with others or by myself? Do I encourage the people around me? Do I treat men and women equally?

- Jesus demonstrates the capacity to develop and maintain lasting friendships. Do you think the ability to share deep friendship with others is a distinguishing mark of being a Christian or a minister?

- "Faithful friends are a sturdy shelter; whoever finds one finds a treasure. Faithful friends are beyond price, no amount can balance their worth." What kind of friendships do you foster? Who would describe you as a faithful friend?

Acts of the Apostles
As Stories of Faith and History

Throughout this book we have examined many interesting and intriguing stories found in Acts of the Apostles. We have entered the world of various (predominantly less familiar) characters and at times re-created scenes and filled in missing details of the narrative.[37] We have not, however, addressed the issue of the book's authorship. Who was this storyteller whose work has inspired countless believers down through the ages? Without this precious account, the stories of early Christianity and its origins would not have been known. The whole canonical Scripture would have been incomplete. The bridge between the Gospels and the Letters of Paul would not have been smooth. Furthermore, the Gospel of Luke would have been inadequate since Luke and Acts (usually labeled as Luke-Acts) are a unit that is meant to be read together as one narrative plot.

It is time now to examine the authorship of this magnificent book. We will also look at the purpose of the book and the reasons the author decided to write this important theological and historical sequel. Through the example of his diligence and hard work, we are encouraged to balance work and leisure as an important trait of a healthy spirituality. But before we hear Luke tell why he decided to write Acts, let us first pause to read his preface, found in Acts 1:1–8:

....

[37] Literary critics call these missing details the "narrative gaps."

In the first book, Theophilus, I dealt with all that Jesus did and taught until the day he was taken up, after giving instructions through the holy Spirit to the apostles whom he had chosen. He presented himself alive to them by many proofs after he had suffered, appearing to them during forty days and speaking about the kingdom of God. While meeting with them, he enjoined them not to depart from Jerusalem, but to wait for "the promise of the Father about which you have heard me speak; for John baptized with water, but in a few days you will be baptized with the holy Spirit."

When they had gathered together they asked him, "Lord, are you at this time going to restore the kingdom to Israel?" He answered them, "It is not for you to know the times or seasons that the Father has established by his own authority. But you will receive power when the holy Spirit comes upon you, and you will be my witnesses in Jerusalem, throughout Judea and Samaria, and to the ends of the earth."

Luke the Storyteller

1. Why did I decide to write Acts?

My name is Luke. I am the Evangelist who wrote the third Gospel. Some might know that I also wrote the Acts of the Apostles, which is a sequel to the Gospel. A clue is also found in the preface of my second volume, which is addressed to the same Theophilus, to whom I dedicated the Gospel. While *Theophilus*, which literally means "a friend of God," was the rich Roman patron who financed my research and writing projects, the two-part story of Christian origins is really dedicated to anyone who is a friend of God.

You might ask, "Why a sequel?" Acts continues the story of human salvation and Christian origins. While the Gospel is about the life, ministry, death, and resurrection of our Savior Jesus Christ, Acts of the Apostles depicts various characters who, like Jesus their founder, are models of Christian discipleship and mission. Two representative figures dominate the book: Peter (chapters 1–12) and Paul (chapters 13–28). While Peter's ministry is to the Jewish people in Jerusalem and Judea, Paul's mission is to Hellenistic Jews and gentiles from Palestine to Asia Minor and even to the capital of the Roman Empire.

The geographical movement of the Christian mission from Galilee to Jerusalem and then to the ends of the world is programmed by God, who declares, "You will be my witnesses in Jerusalem, throughout Judea and Samaria, and to the ends of the earth." Thus, just as God's great promises to Israel have been fulfilled in the life and mission of Jesus, the hand of God was also behind the mission of the early Church. The universal mission that extends to the farthest corners of the world and includes both Jews and gentiles is part of God's great plan for Israel and humanity. Everything that takes place in history happens according to the will and purpose of God.[38]

> **Sidebar 10.1**
> **Biblical Characters**
>
> **Who was...*St. Luke*?**
>
> ❖ He was the Evangelist who traditionally has been credited as the author of the Gospel of Luke and the Acts of the Apostles, which is clearly meant to be read as a sequel to the Gospel account.
>
> ❖ He was believed to be a native of Antioch. The "we-sections" (passages in Acts written in the first person plural) seem to indicate that the author (Luke) was traveling with Paul during parts of his missionary journeys.
>
> ❖ Tradition claims that he was a physician (see Col 4:14). He was Paul's co-worker and faithful friend (Phlm 24; 2 Tm 4:11)
>
> ❖ He is often depicted in art as an ox or bull, usually having wings. The ox is a traditional symbol representing the Gospel of Luke.
>
> ❖ He is the patron of students, artists, and physicians. His feast day is October 18.

....

[38] While this theology might strike us as predestination, it is generally recognized as a Lukan theology.

In a sense, Acts of the Apostles develops theological themes already introduced in the Gospel. The prefaces of the Gospel (1:1–4) and of Acts (1:1–2) point to the literary unity of both works. Moreover, the ending of the Gospel leads smoothly into the beginning of Acts, resuming various theological themes and events: proof of the Lord's resurrection (Luke 24:36–43; Acts 1:3); the commissioning of the apostles to be witnesses of the resurrection (Luke 24:48; Acts 1:8); instructions to wait in Jerusalem for the gift of the Spirit (Luke 24:49; Acts 1:4–5); and accounts of the Lord's ascension (Luke 24:50–53; Acts 1:9). Since Luke-Acts narrates a single story of redemptive history, both volumes are symbiotically related and are meant to be read together as a unified narrative. Consequently, some of you scholars have keenly noticed the geographical movement found in Luke-Acts. The Gospel is divided into a three-part geographical structure outlined in Luke 1:1–2:

Luke 1:1–9:50	in Galilee
Luke 9:51–19:44	on the way to Jerusalem
Luke 19:45–24:53	in Jerusalem

Acts of the Apostles picks up where the Gospel left off and is also divided into a three-part geographical structure as outlined in Acts 1:8, "You will be my witnesses in Jerusalem, throughout Judea and Samaria, and to the ends of the earth":

Acts 1:1–6:7	in Jerusalem
Acts 6:8–12:25	in Judea and Samaria
Acts 13:1–28:31	to the ends of the earth

Unfortunately, the canonical arrangement of your Bible caused my two volumes to be separated by the presence of John's Gospel. From a canonical perspective, this makes perfect sense, since Acts functions as a bridge between the four Gospels and the story of the Church. Furthermore, Acts provides a very good framework for reading Paul and other authors of apostolic epistles.

However, it is my intention that Luke and Acts be read together as a unified narrative.

Many stylistic and theological clues indicate that these two volumes have one theological vision. The Gospel begins with the birth of Jesus; Acts, with the birth of the Church. The Spirit descends on Jesus after prayer (Luke 3:22), the Spirit pours out on the disciples after their prayers (Acts 2:1–13). The Gospel describes the mission and ministry of Jesus, Acts outlines the mission and ministry of the early Church. There are many other striking parallels between the two volumes that have not gone unnoticed by you fine biblical scholars, such as the parallel trials of Jesus and Paul. Each of them is found innocent in all four cases.

In general, what is foretold in the Gospel will be accomplished in Acts, and what happened to Jesus will also be experienced by the disciples. One notable motif that recurs frequently is prayer. In Luke's Gospel, Jesus prays frequently, especially during critical moments of his life and passion. Jesus prayed at baptism (3:21), in deserted places (5:16), before choosing the Twelve (6:12), in solitude (9:18, 28), to the Father (11:2), for Peter before his denial (22:32), before the passion (22:42), and on the cross (23:34). What Jesus did, the apostles and disciples imitated. The disciples prayed in the upper room (Acts 1:14), before choosing a successor to Judas (1:24), and in communal life (2:42, 46, 47). Acts reports the disciples constantly at prayer: Peter and John prayed in the temple (3:1), Ananias hears the Lord before receiving Paul (9:11), Peter prayed at midday in Joppa (10:9), Cornelius received a vision while praying (10:4), Paul and Barnabas prayed over the appointed elders (14:23). In times of trials and persecution, Paul often turned to prayer for strength and courage (16:25; 20:36; 21:5; 22:17). In a nutshell, prayer functions three ways in Luke-Acts: (1) a means to know God's will and purpose, (2) a source of power to do God's will, and (3) a catalyst for God to accomplish God's divine plan and intention. Thus to be a disciple, one must pray constantly, just as Jesus prayed.

2. Who am I?

Many things have been said about me over the years. Some of the traditions are true, while others are more legendary. For example, because of my basic knowledge of medical terms and graphic descriptions of some of the healings, people think I am a doctor. The reference about me being a "beloved physician" in the Letter to the Colossians (4:14) augmented my reputation tremendously. To tell you the truth, I am no doctor. Having been trained in Greco-Roman rhetoric and higher education, I am simply well versed in medical terms, just as I am with nautical matters. Plus, since Greek is my native tongue, writing about these things is second nature to me.

I am a gentile second-generation Christian from Antioch. I had the privilege of traveling with the great Apostle Paul on some of his missionary journeys. The so-called "we-sections" in Acts (16:10–17; 20:5–15; 21:1–18; 27:1 – 28:16) are obvious clues that I was among Paul's company on those occasions. Although some modern scholars think the "we-sections" is only a literary device used in ancient biographies to show the veracity of the account, these sections actually came from a diary I kept while traveling with Paul and his company. Of course I might have added a few things here and there to make the story more interesting and to help the transition of the narrative, but much of the account comes directly from my travel log.

I have always been honored to be associated with the great Apostle Paul, who considered me his co-worker in his Letter to Philemon (v. 24). I was even with him in his imprisonment (2 Timothy 4:11). I do not know everything about the life of Paul, nor did I intend to give an account of his total vision of Christianity. What I have attempted to do in Acts of the Apostles is to capture the basic contours of his theology and mission from my own perspective within the theological framework of the two volumes. As a result, my chronology of Paul's life and theology might differ somewhat from Paul's own letters. It is therefore important to realize that Acts is not meant to be strictly an historical account in the modern sense.

3. When and where was Acts written?

Acts chronicles in selective fashion the period of 30–64 CE. Twenty years have passed since the death of Peter and Paul, and the Church has changed significantly since then. The Gospel of Mark has been written, which Matthew and I have used to elaborate our version of the Good News of Jesus Christ for our own communities. Soon after the Gospel was completed, I was commissioned to continue the sequel. After having investigated everything accurately and interviewing all the living eyewitnesses, I began to arrange everything into "an orderly sequence" (Luke 1:3). Thanks to the inspiration of the Holy Spirit, I was able to finish the project fairly quickly. The year was about 85, in Antioch on the Orontes River in Syria (modern-day Turkey).

Sidebar 10.2
Biblical Backgrounds

What is...*parousia*?

❖ It is a Greek word for "presence, arrival, or official visit." But it is also a Christian theological concept and belief referring to the Second Coming of Christ.

❖ This anticipated second return of Jesus Christ is based on prophecies found in many New Testament writings. The time of the Second Coming is spoken of as "that day" (2 Tm 4:8), "the day of the Lord" (1 Thes 5:2), "the day of Christ Jesus" (Phil 1:6), "the day the Son of Man is revealed" (Lk 17:30), and "the last day" (Jn 6:39–40). New Testament writers stressed much about the last day. Their thoughts and ideas are called eschatology.

❖ The Nicene Creed includes the following belief about Jesus: "He will come again in glory to judge the living and the dead and his kingdom will have no end."

❖ Concerning the time, Jesus clearly warned, "It is not for you to know the times or seasons that the Father has established by his own authority" (Acts 1:7).

4. *What sort of book is Acts?*

Since the genre of Acts is unique in ancient literature, many scholars have unfortunately misunderstood my intent in writing this second volume. So let me start by stating what Acts is not. First, it is not a novel or even an historical novel written purely for entertainment as some of you have erroneously claimed. Second, even though my prefaces bear some striking resemblances to the prefaces of ancient works like Polybius, Josephus, and Philo, Acts is not a scientific treatise nor does it completely resemble ancient biographies of famous philosophers and heroes. Unlike the Gospel, which is largely a biography of the life of Jesus, Acts does not focus on any particular character; rather, it records the history of a rising movement—the movement of the followers of Jesus.

Before putting pen to paper, I investigated everything accurately, as I had done for the first volume. But more than just recording historical facts like your modern history books, I also wanted to unveil how the promises of God and the prophecies of Scripture "have been fulfilled among us" (Luke 1:1). To effectively accomplish this two-fold task of recording a narrative of the Church's theological and historical beginnings, I have decided to fuse together various ancient genres. The closest and most accurate categorization is a "historiography" with an apologetic aim. In your terminology, you might call it a hybrid of history and hagiography.

The real reason I have chosen to write this volume using this type of mixed genre of "historiography" is because multiple and complex issues are emerging that need to be addressed. First and foremost, there is a need to show that the promises in the Hebrew Scriptures and of Jesus are fulfilled in the Church. Second, since the Church has become increasingly diverse, I want to offer a vision that would help you become more unified, together with a theology of mission that propels you into the future while you wait for the *parousia*—the Second Coming of Christ. Third, as the Church becomes more gentile, there is a need to explain how gentile Christians are legitimate heirs of God's promises. Finally, with increased tension and persecution from Roman authorities, there is a need to show that Christianity is a peaceful movement that causes no political threat to the Establishment. Consequently, with these goals, I hope that as you read the narrative of the Acts of the Apostles, you will come to know better who you are and where you have come from. Furthermore, as you enter the world of the characters, may they inspire you to respond boldly and faithfully.

Balancing Work and Leisure

It must have taken Luke a lot of time, energy, and effort to investigate everything and to write both the Gospel and the Acts of the Apostles. His two volumes together make up 27 percent of the New Testament. I have always wondered how he was able to accomplish so much. He must have had a very strong work ethic, yet he seemed to know how to enjoy life and liked traveling. The depiction of Jesus as one who likes to dine and eat with friends and outcasts might actually reflect Luke's own character. Furthermore, Jesus is constantly on the road in a section in the Gospel, which scholars call "the travel narrative," found in Luke 9:51—19:27. Acts also contains many stories of meals and travel narratives. Paul had three missionary journeys, and Luke accompanied him on that part of the journey known as the "we-section" in Acts. These examples indicate that Luke the Evangelist seems to have a well-balanced spirituality of work and leisure.

But what exactly is work? What do we mean by leisure? How are these important components of today's spirituality? Contemporary spiritual writers have stressed the importance of the connection between leisure and spirituality. In his popular book, *By Way of the Heart: Toward a Holistic Christian Spirituality*, Wilkie Au writes, "Any spirituality that leaves out leisure will lack depth and balance because leisure lies at the heart of prayer, community, and friendship."[39] Similarly, in her book *Traits of a Healthy Spirituality,* Melannie Svoboda states, "I believe that a wholesome attitude toward both work and leisure is integral to our Christian faith—so much so, that I do not hesitate to designate 'the balancing of work and leisure' as one more trait of a healthy spirituality."[40]

We are created for both work and leisure. Work stimulates our mind, engages our body, energizes our creativity, and helps us make an impact on the world in which we live. Work is a gift for the body and soul. Without work, our body becomes restless and our spirit becomes stagnant. But leisure is as important to our human existence as work. Work without leisure robs us of our joy, freezes our imagination, and strips us of the desire to create. Leisure is the necessary counterpart to work. The problem is that many people do not recognize the relationship between leisure and spiritual wellness.

Rest and leisure are rare commodities in today's modern and technological world. In a society like the United of States of America, which is so oriented toward work and productivity, leisure is a difficult thing for many people. Perhaps that is why I find many Americans who are overworked and stressed out. I must admit that the environment I live in has also influenced my life. As a scholar, I too am a victim of the pursuit-of-excellence syndrome and at times have fallen into a "workaholic" lifestyle. I have often over-extended myself in attempting to avoid perishing from a lack of publications. I have often traveled to national and international destinations to give papers and lectures to help improve my credentials. As a result, there were times I neglected

....

[39] Wilkie Au, SJ, *By Way of the Heart: Toward a Holistic Christian Spirituality* (New York/Mahwah: Paulist Press,1989), 39.

[40] Svoboda, *Traits,* 81–82.

friends, community life, health and spiritual well-being to enhance work productivity.

Unfortunately, many people do not realize that excessive work can destroy the holistic balance in one's life and can ultimately lead to a breakdown in one's spirituality and relationships. People who are addicted to their work and in the helping professions are prime candidates for being in a state of joyless exhaustion, popularly known as "burnout." Many ministers, both religious and lay, struggle with taking time off for prayer, rest, and recreation. Their life completely revolves around helping others, and they reluctantly take time off for leisure. Taking time off to rest is often a low priority on their list of things to do.

Believe it or not, the Bible speaks much about work and rest. In the beginning, God was quite busy, creating the sun and the moon, the earth and the stars, mountains and valleys, seas and rivers, and all living creatures. Everything came into being through God's powerful commands. God said, "Let there be light," and there was. "Let there be mountains and seas," and there were. But that is in the first Creation story (Genesis 1). In the second Creation story (Genesis 2), God did not just create through a spoken word. God actually got down on his knees, took a lump of clay, and worked with his hands to form Adam. God carefully sculpted Adam and blew life into his nostrils. Like a gardener, God actually planted trees and plants, and then placed Adam in the garden so he could enjoy its beauty and eat its fruits. God did not just work and work. At the end of each day of creation, God pronounced it to be "very good," and then God rested. God actually took time out to delight in what God had made. On the seventh day, when everything was completely finished, God rested. Just as God rested on the seventh day, Israel was also commanded to follow.

The seventh day of the week is called the Sabbath, which in Hebrew literally means "cessation or rest." The Sabbath is a day of rest consecrated to the Lord. God explicitly commanded, "Remember the sabbath day—keep it holy" (Exodus 20:8). The Torah has many prescriptions concerning the Sabbath; all work is forbidden, for Israelites as well as for strangers and beasts. Some examples of activities prohibited on the Sabbath are cooking, plowing, reaping, lighting a fire, trading, gathering, and loading animals, just to name a few. Willful violation of the Sabbath observance was punishable by death (Exodus 31:14–15).

As a Jew, Jesus must have observed the Sabbath. However, he was more flexible with its rules and regulations. He acted against the absurd rigidity of the law. He criticized the scribes and Pharisees for placing an intolerable burden on people's shoulders (Matthew 23:4), and proclaimed that "the Sabbath was made for man, not man for the Sabbath" (Mark 2:27). He cured on the Sabbath and defended his disciples for plucking ears of corn on that day. He argued that the Sabbath is not broken in cases of necessity or by acts of charity (Matthew 12:3; Mark 2:25; Luke 6:3). Jesus definitely worked hard, so hard that he got exhausted. On one occasion, when people were coming and going in great numbers, he and his disciples did not even have an opportunity to eat and rest. Jesus said to his weary disciples, "Come away by yourselves to a deserted place and rest a while" (Mark 6:31).

Jesus, too, had to balance his work with rest and leisure. In the Gospel of Luke, Jesus dines regularly. It is said that in this Gospel, Jesus is either going to or coming from a dinner party. But Jesus also prays frequently, especially at crucial moments in his life: at his baptism, before choosing the Twelve, at the Transfiguration, in the garden of Gethsemane, and on the cross. Luke specifically stated that Jesus "would withdraw to deserted places to pray" (5:16). Jesus certainly saw the need to retreat to quiet places to be in communion with God and "recharge" his human energy. Jesus knows the difficulty of living. There are moments when we do not know where to go and to whom we can turn. Life seems to be at an impasse. To those who find life weighted down with stress and anxiety, Jesus appeals to them, saying, "Come to me, all you who labor and are burdened, and I will give you rest. Take my yoke upon you and learn from me, for I am meek and humble of heart; and you will find rest for yourselves. For my yoke is easy, and my burden light" (Matthew 11:28–30). Allow me to conclude with a prayer:

Lord God,
creator of the universe,
I rejoice that you can make all things new,
from chaos to order,
from weariness to strength.

Give me the grace
to trust you
to be still with you
to experience renewed love and inspiration,
fresh courage and determination.

Help me to balance work and leisure in my daily life.

Give me a healthy disposition toward work
and a wholesome spirit toward leisure.

May I always be open to the guidance of the Holy Spirit
to embrace new possibilities
and to follow you in whichever direction you lead.

May I never be afraid of the unknown
as I journey to you, who is known.

Amen.

Points for Reflection

- One of the primary reasons Luke wrote Luke-Acts is to show that God has fulfilled his promises. How is God fulfilling his promises in you and through you? Take time to be still and recall how God has been there for you along the way.

- The motif of prayer is repeated throughout Luke-Acts. What Jesus did, the apostles also followed. How important has your prayer life been? Do you need to retreat to a deserted place and rest a while with Jesus?

- Quite often in Scripture, God's work is described as removing the old and replacing it with the new: "See, I am creating new heavens and a new earth" (Isaiah 65:17); "From their bodies I will remove the hearts of stone, and give them hearts of flesh" (Ezekiel 11:19); "A clean heart create for me, God; renew within me a steadfast spirit" (Psalm 51:12); "the kingdom of heaven is like the head of a household who brings from his storeroom both the new and the old" (Matthew 13:52). Which one of these quotes touches you the most and why?

- What is your attitude toward work and leisure? What are some concrete ways you are trying to balance work and leisure in your life? For a change, give yourself one hour of leisure every day and experience your leisure differently each day. Try things like taking a walk, sitting in a park, reading a book, hiking up a mountain, writing a poem, having coffee with a friend, planning a trip, picking up a new hobby or sport.

Conclusion

Acts of the Apostles recounts the miraculous and unpredictable working of the Holy Spirit in the lives of real people. Some are very well known in the Church's traditions. Peter, the apostle to the Jews and pillar of the church in Jerusalem, dominates the first half of the book, while Paul, the apostle to the gentiles, is the main character in the latter part of the book. But there are also inspiring stories of ordinary believers who are often overlooked.

This book, *Stories of Early Christianity*, took ten important events found in Acts of the Apostles and retold them in an imaginative style. Most of the stories were done through character narration. However, two were in an interview format, and one in the form of a letter. In different creative styles and formats, the characters recounted their spiritual and faith journeys in ways that would allow us to be drawn into the stories, identify ourselves with the biblical characters and events, and be transformed in the act of reading. Through the retellings, we have discovered a whole new list of extraordinary individuals who have often gone unnoticed: Mary, the patient mother; Matthias, the prayerful apostle; Rhoda, the joyful servant; John Mark, the reconciler; Cornelius, the faith-seeker; Barnabas, the encourager; Lydia, the persistent hostess; Dionysius, the open-minded Areopagite; Priscilla, the migrant missionary "apostle"; and Luke, the masterful storyteller.

Furthermore, through these creative retellings of faith and history, we were able to uncover some seemingly unsolved mysteries of the Bible. In her retelling of Pentecost, Rhoda places the event in the upper room of the house of Mary, the mother of John

Mark, who had a house in Jerusalem. Her account is based on a well-supported historical reconstruction. In the story of Priscilla and Aquila, we are informed that the couple was expelled from Rome by the Edict of Claudius in the year 49. The real reason for their expulsion was because they were likely "ringleaders" of the Christian movement in Rome. Moreover, since they arrived in Corinth before Paul, they were probably the founders of the church there. They later moved to Ephesus and probably founded the church there as well. After the death of the emperor Claudius, they eventually returned to their home in Rome. But that is not all. The migrant couple was co-workers of Paul and mentors of the great preacher Apollos. A fragmentary description from Second Timothy (4:19) indicates that the couple later returned to Ephesus to minister to the community there and became collaborators with the young Timothy. In the story about the first European convert, we discover that the Macedonian man who appeared in Paul's vision was not the first European convert, but rather it was Lydia, who was a gentile "God-fearer" and a businesswoman in purple dye from Thyatira.

In the retellings, we have also discovered the manner in which Paul went about establishing his communities. When he arrived in a city or town, Paul rented out a storefront shop on the ground floor, with living quarters on the floor above. These types of tenement buildings were called *insulae* (plural), or *insula* (singular). While practicing his trade or business as leatherworker or tentmaker, Paul preached the Christian message to clients, customers, and curious passersby. These are just a few examples of historical reconstructions revealed in these creative retellings. Consequently, *Stories of Early Christianity* is not a work of fiction but is grounded on textual evidence and archaeological findings.

The book is not unrelated to the Christian life today. It fosters ten important traits of healthy spirituality for contemporary Christians. Drawn from the biblical reflections, the following themes were explored and examined: "being still"; prayer; joy; forgiveness; openness; encouragement; gratitude; tolerance of diversity; friendship; and balancing work and leisure.

As a way to conclude this book, allow me to say a few more words about Acts of the Apostles. The author of Acts narrates interesting events under intriguing circumstances. Acts has something for everyone: tongues of fire (2:3), healings (3:1–10), deception (5:1–6), massive conversion (2:41), avenging angels (12:23), earthquakes (16:26), shipwrecks (27:41–44), harrowing escapes (9:23–25; 21:30–36), riots (19:23–40), murderous plots (9:23; 23:12–15; 25:1–3), political intrigue (16:35–39; 22:24–29; 24:26–27), courtroom drama (23:1–10), exorcism (19:13–17), snake bites (28:1–6), and so much more. Acts even has humor, which is not commonly found in the New Testament. After having escaped from prison, Peter, who was a fugitive, was left at the gate because Rhoda—the maid—was too overcome with joy to let him in (12:13–16). Paul got carried away and spoke all night long, causing a young man who was sitting on the windowsill on the third floor to fall asleep and fall out of the window and die. After having restored his life by literally lying on him, Paul resumed his sermon as if nothing had happened (20:7–12).

The stories in Acts have the flair of an exciting adventure novel to which we can relate. These stories represent moments in the early years of the Christian movement that are worthy to be passed on and remembered. More than just a simple collection of "good stories," Acts of the Apostles reports the history of the origins of the Church that is filled with theological, spiritual, and pastoral significance. Furthermore, these stories are told in interesting ways so that we are drawn into the action and transformed by it. We might find ourselves wondering what we might say and how we might respond in similar circumstances. Like Peter, for example, we might resist going into their homes and eating with people who are ethnically different. On the other hand, we might be like Paul who is more flexible about cultural and geographical restrictions. Or having heard Peter's speech at Pentecost, we might ask the same question the inhabitants of Jerusalem once asked, "What are we to do?" (2:37)

From beginning to end, Acts is a narrative of surprise. The events and activities of the early Church are directly connected with the work of the Holy Spirit, who is often unpredictable and always uncontrollable. Filled with the Spirit, the characters in Acts often do unexpected things and give unrehearsed responses. Acts even has an open-ended, surprise ending. The Word of God was unhindered and continued to be preached to the ends of the earth. Perhaps the open-ended conclusion is meant to call us to continue in that mission.

Bibliography

Ascough, Richard S. *Lydia: Paul's Cosmopolitan Hostess.* Paul's Social Network: Brothers and Sisters in Faith; Collegeville, MN: Liturgical Press, 2009.

Au, Wilkie, SJ. *By Way of the Heart: Toward a Holistic Christian Spirituality.* New York/Mahwah: Paulist Press, 1989.

Castle, Anthony. *A Treasure of Quips, Quotes, and Anecdotes for Preachers and Teachers.* Mystic, CT: Twenty-third Publications, 1998.

Colquhoun, Frank. *Prayers for Today.* Philadelphia, PA: Triangle Publications, 1989.

Downey, Michael. *Understanding Christian Spirituality.* New York: Paulist Press, 1997.

Fitzmyer, Joseph A. *The Acts of the Apostles.* Anchor Bible; New York: Doubleday, 1998.

Gallagher, Robert L., and Hertig, Paul, eds. *Mission in Acts: Ancient Narratives in Contemporary Context.* Maryknoll, NY: Orbis Books, 2004.

Grün, Anselm. *Images of Jesus.* New York: Continuum, 2002.

Hartin, Patrick J. *Apollos: Paul's Partner or Rival?* Paul's Social Network: Brothers and Sisters in Faith; Collegeville, MN: Liturgical Press, 2009.

Johnson, Luke Timothy. *The Acts of the Apostles.* Sacra Pagina; Collegeville, MN: Liturgical Press, 1992.

Kee, H. C. *Good News to the Ends of the Earth: The Theology of Acts.* Philadelphia: Trinity/London: SCM, 1990.

Keller, Marie Noël. *Priscilla and Aquila: Paul's Co-workers in Christ Jesus.* Paul's Social Network: Brothers and Sisters in Faith; Collegeville, MN: Liturgical Press, 2010.

Malina, Bruce J. *Timothy: Paul's Closest Associate.* Paul's Social Network: Brothers and Sisters in Faith; Collegeville, MN: Liturgical Press, 2008.

Marshall, I. Howard, and Peterson, David, eds. *Witness to the Gospel: The Theology of Acts.* Grand Rapids, MI: Eerdmans, 1998.

Miles, Margaret R. *Practicing Christianity: Critical Perspectives for an Embodied Spirituality.* New York: Crossroad, 1988.

Nguyen, vanThanh, SVD. "An Asian View of Biblical Hospitality (Luke 10:5–8)." *Biblical Research* 53 (2008) 25–39.

_____. "Asia in Motion: A Biblical Reflection on Migration." *Asian Christian Review* 4.2 (Winter 2010) 18–31.

_____. Dismantling Cultural Boundaries: Missiological Implications of Acts 10:1—11:18." *Missiology: An International Review* 40.4 (October 2012) 455-66.

_____. *Peter and Cornelius: A Story of Conversion and Mission.* Eugene, OR: Pickwick Publications, 2012.

Peck, M. Scott, MD. *The Road Less Traveled: A New Psychology of Love, Traditional Values and Spiritual Growth.* 25th Anniversary Edition; New York: Simon & Schuster, 1978/2002.

Svoboda, Melannie, SND. *Traits of a Healthy Spirituality.* Mystic, CT: Twenty-Third Publications, 1997.

Tannehill, Robert C. *The Narrative Unity of Luke-Acts: A Literary Interpretation.* Vol. 2. Philadelphia: Fortress, 1990.

Williamson, Charles C. *Acts.* Interpretation Bible Studies; Louisville, KY: Westminster John Knox Press, 2000.

Winter, Bruce W. *Roman Wives, Roman Widows: The Appearance of New Women and the Pauline Communities.* Grand Rapids, MI: Eerdmans, 2003.

Witherington III, B. *The Acts of the Apostles: A Socio-Rhetorical Commentary.* Grand Rapids, MI: Eerdmans, 1998.

About the Author

vanThanh Nguyen, SVD, SThD, is associate professor of New Testament studies and the director of the master of divinity program at Catholic Theological Union in Chicago, Illinois. He is also the author of *Peter and Cornelius: A Story of Conversion and Mission* (Pickwick, 2012).